MAKERSPACES IN LIBRARIES

Library Technology Essentials

About the Series

The *Library Technology Essentials* series helps librarians utilize today's hottest new technologies as well as ready themselves for tomorrow's. The series features titles that cover the A–Z of how to leverage the latest and most cutting-edge technologies and trends to deliver new library services.

Today's forward-thinking libraries are responding to changes in information consumption, new technological advancements, and growing user expectations by devising groundbreaking ways to remain relevant in a rapidly changing digital world. This collection of primers guides libraries along the path to innovation through step-by-step instruction. Written by the field's top experts, these handbooks serve as the ultimate gateway to the newest and most promising emerging technology trends. Filled with practical advice and projects for libraries to implement right now, these books inspire readers to start leveraging these new techniques and tools today.

About the Series Editor

Ellyssa Kroski is the Director of Information Technology at the New York Law Institute as well as an award-winning editor and author of 22 books including *Law Librarianship in the Digital Age* for which she won the AALL's 2014 Joseph L. Andrews Legal Literature Award. Her ten-book technology series, The Tech Set, won the ALA's Best Book in Library Literature Award in 2011. She is a librarian, an adjunct faculty member at Pratt Institute, and an international conference speaker. She speaks at several conferences a year, mainly about new tech trends, digital strategy, and libraries.

Titles in the Series

1. *Wearable Technology: Smart Watches to Google Glass for Libraries*, by Tom Bruno
2. *MOOCs and Libraries*, by Kyle K. Courtney
3. *Free Technology for Libraries*, by Amy Deschenes
4. *Makerspaces in Libraries*, by Theresa Willingham and Jeroen De Boer
5. *Knowledge Management for Libraries*, by Valerie Forrestal
6. *WordPress for Libraries*, by Chad Haefele
7. *Game It Up! Using Gamification to Incentivize Your Library*, by David Folmar
8. *Data Visualizations and Infographics*, by Sarah K. C. Mauldin
9. *Mobile Social Marketing in Libraries*, by Samantha C. Helmick
10. *Digital Collections and Exhibits*, by Juan Denzer
11. *Using Tablets and Apps in Libraries*, by Elizabeth Willse
12. *Responsive Web Design in Practice*, by Jason A. Clark

MAKERSPACES IN LIBRARIES

Theresa Willingham and Jeroen De Boer

ROWMAN & LITTLEFIELD
Lanham • Boulder • New York • London

Published by Rowman & Littlefield
A wholly owned subsidary of The Rowman & Littlefield Publishing Group,
Inc.
4501 Forbes Boulevard, Suite 200, Lanham, Maryland 20706
www.rowman.com

Unit A, Whitacre Mews, 26-34 Stannary Street, London SE11 4AB

British Library Cataloguing in Publication Information Available

Library of Congress Cataloging-in-Publication Data

Willingham, Theresa.
Makerspaces in libraries / Theresa Willingham and Jeroen DeBoer.
pages cm. – (Library technology essentials ; 4)
Includes bibliographical references and index.
ISBN 978-1-4422-5299-8 (cloth : alk. paper) – ISBN 978-1-4422-5300-1 (pbk. : alk. paper) – ISBN
978-1-4422-5301-8 (ebook)
1. Libraries–Activity programs. 2. Libraries and community. 3. Makerspaces. 4. Do-it-yourself
work. 5. Workshops. I. DeBoer, Jeroen, 1973- II. Title.
Z716.33.W55 2015
025.5–dc23
2015011912

∞ ™ The paper used in this publication meets the minimum requirements of
American National Standard for Information Sciences Permanence of Paper
for Printed Library Materials, ANSI/NISO Z39.48-1992.

Printed in the United States of America

The library in 2020 will be ruled by geeks. In my happy vision for the future, libraries are ruled by benign geek librarian overlords and the world is full of awesome.
—Sarah Houghton

CONTENTS

Series Editor's Foreword   ix

Preface   xiii

Acknowledgments   xv

1   An Introduction to Makerspaces   1

2   Getting Started with Makerspaces   11

3   Tools and Applications   29

4   Library Examples and Case Studies   39

5   Step-by-Step Library Projects   69

6   Tips and Tricks   119

7   Future Trends   125

Recommended Reading   129

Index   133

About the Authors   141

SERIES EDITOR'S FOREWORD

Makerspaces, hackerspaces, and FabLabs have become enormously popular community hubs where people gather to "make" and create everything from 3D printed objects to sewn garments to software applications. *Makerspaces in Libraries* is an all-in-one passport to these intriguing spaces, providing libraries with instructions for what it takes to run a library makerspace and develop programming, including tackling everything from planning and budgeting to staff training and best practices. Makerspace experts Theresa Willingham and Jeroen de Boer deftly guide readers through a jam-packed projects chapter that will transform any library into a state-of-the-art maker hub. Projects range from 3D printing, laser cutting, and robotics, to creating Arduino lights and hosting hackathons, and are geared for all types of patrons from kids to seniors.

The idea for the Library Technology Essentials book series came about because there have been many drastic changes in information consumption, new technological advancements, and growing user expectations over the past few years, which forward-thinking libraries are responding to by devising groundbreaking ways to remain relevant in a rapidly changing digital world. I saw a need for a practical set of guidebooks that libraries could use to inform themselves about how to stay on the cutting edge by implementing new programs, services, and technologies to match their patrons' expectations.

Libraries today are embracing new and emerging technologies, transforming themselves into community hubs and places of co-creation through makerspaces, developing information commons spaces, and even taking on new roles and formats, all the while searching for ways to decrease budget lines, add value, and prove the return on investment of the library. The Library Technology Essentials series is a collection of primers to guide libraries along the path to innovation through step-by-step instruction. Written by the field's top experts, these handbooks are meant to serve as the ultimate gateway to the newest and most promising emerging technology trends. Filled with practical advice and project ideas for libraries to implement right now, these books will hopefully inspire readers to start leveraging these new techniques and tools today.

Each book follows the same format and outline, guiding the reader through the A to Z of how to leverage the latest and most cutting-edge technologies and trends to deliver new library services. The "Projects" chapter constitutes the largest portion of the books, providing library initiatives that can be implemented by both beginner and advanced readers and accommodating for all audiences and levels of technical expertise. These projects and programs range from the basic "How to Circulate Wearable Technology in Your Library" and "How to Host a *FIRST* Robotics Team at the Library" to intermediate such as "How to Create a Hands-Free Digital Exhibit Showcase with Microsoft Kinect" to the more advanced options such as "Implementing a Scalable E-Resources Management System" and "How to Gamify Library Orientation for Patrons with a Top Down Video Game." Readers of all skill levels will find something of interest in these books.

Theresa Willingham and Jeroen de Boer have each been working in and helping to build makerspaces in libraries for several years. After hearing about Jeroen's work with mobile FabLabs such as FryskLab in the Netherlands and Terri's work developing makerspaces, maker festivals, and *FIRST* STEM education programs, I just knew that these two had to team up to write a book on makerspaces. This super duo brings their expansive knowledge and practical expertise to this outstanding resource providing invaluable instruction and wisdom for designing and providing programming for makerspaces in libraries.

Ellyssa Kroski
Director of Information Technology
The New York Law Institute
http://www.ellyssakroski.com

PREFACE

Makerspaces—interactive, multifunctional spaces for creative exploration, design, and development—are increasingly popular in both public and academic libraries as a new way to engage patrons and add value to traditional library services. From planning your innovation center to hosting hack-a-thons, guest lectures, game nights, and maker-style social events, this practical primer provides detailed guidance and best practices for creating an enduring, community-driven space for all to enjoy and from which both staff and patrons will benefit.

This well-researched, in-depth guide to makerspace planning and development will serve libraries of all sizes seeking to implement the latest technologies and adopt the newest trends in their libraries in thoughtful, nuanced, and enduring ways. Written from the perspective and experience of space users, as well as facility designers and developers, *Makerspaces in Libraries* provides user-friendly, practical, and creative treatment of the benefits and challenges of creating a library-based makerspace, presented in an enjoyable, unintimidating, and inspiring format.

Starting with a comprehensive overview of the history of makerspaces generally and in libraries specifically, in chapter 1, the book goes on, in chapters 2 and 3, to an exploration of essential documentation, tools, and applications. Chapter 4 takes an in-depth look at library makerspace case studies from around the United States and Europe to glean best practices and recommendations from librarians experienced in makerspace and FabLab development and operation. Chapter 5 takes you into the heart of what it means to be a "maker," with a series of fun and interesting step-by-step, hands-on projects on everything from learning about 3D printing with practical printing projects, to starting a *FIRST* youth robotics team in your library, to engaging senior makers with "Squishy Circuits." Chapter 6 brings it all together with "Best Practices for Creating an Agile and Enduring Library Maker-space." Chapter 7 looks at potential future trends and is followed by a bibliographic recommended reading list.

Taken altogether, *Makerspaces in Libraries* is your user-friendly, annotated guide to an exciting new way to bring fresh life and engaging programming to your library and to revitalize your library's place in your community.

ACKNOWLEDGMENTS

This book would not be possible without the professional librarianship, kindness, and generosity of spirit of all the great librarians who shared their stories and expertise, and all the wonderful libraries that shared their resources and guidance. Every library featured here, and every librarian whose words you'll read, is precedent setting in every way, paving the way for twenty-first-century libraries worldwide. The library of the future, like the historical library, is a safe and welcoming place of shared knowledge and a calming sanctuary from a fast-paced world, but also a democratic conduit for active creation and economic productivity. Thank you to all who shared their knowledge with us, so we could share it with you, so you can keep making the future better for all of us.

I

AN INTRODUCTION TO MAKERSPACES

Libraries have always been places for making knowledge, building insight, and launching investigations into the nature of things. Adding a makerspace component to a library is the natural next step to bring innovative learning and productive self-expression to patrons and helps libraries take their rightful place as cultural and creative community hubs. Now, instead of serving as a passive source of archival information, the library can become an active source of skills acquisition and productivity.

Makerspaces, sometimes also referred to as hackerspaces or Fab-Labs, are creative, DIY (do-it-yourself) spaces where people can gather to create, invent, and learn. In libraries they often have 3D printers, software, electronics, craft and hardware supplies and tools, and more. Makerspaces are becoming increasingly popular in both public and academic libraries as a new way to engage patrons and add value to traditional library services.

With this step-by-step guidebook, you'll discover how you can create a makerspace within your own library. From planning your innovation center to hosting hack-a-thons, maker festivals, game nights and build nights, and creative social events in your library, this practical primer provides detailed guidance and best practices.

Makerspaces in Libraries is your handbook to revitalizing your library as a twenty-first-century center of innovation, providing a comprehensive look at the history of makerspaces and their growing influences on libraries, along with practical steps for developing creative spaces and programming in libraries of all sizes.

HISTORY OF MAKERSPACES

The history of the makerspace movement is usually sourced to the European hacker collectives of the late 1990s and early 2000s.[1] One of the first independent hackerspaces to open was c-base in Germany in 1995. Today, c-base is still in operation with a membership of more · than 450 people.[2]

While today "makerspace" and "hackerspace" are often used almost interchangeably, the hacker movement got its start as an open hardware movement advocating greater consumer and user development access to electronic and computer technologies. NYC Resistor and HacDC, in Washington, D.C., both of which opened in 2007, followed by Noisebridge in San Francisco in 2008, were the first U.S. efforts.

The makerspace is the more DIY-oriented cousin of the hackerspace, inspired by *Make:* magazine, which came out in 2005. In 2006, *Make:* hosted the first ever Maker Faire, in San Francisco. "Part science fair, part county fair, and part something entirely new," Maker Faire created a gathering opportunity for tinkers, crafters, hobbyists, artists, and more to come together in a family-friendly environment and made the word "Maker" a new buzzword, if not yet exactly a household name.[3]

In 2013, 195,000 people attended the two flagship Maker Faires in the Bay Area and New York; dozens of smaller regional maker festivals are held nationwide, and hundreds of makerspaces now dot the United States. From neighborhood garages to franchise TechShops, these creative spaces provide opportunities to build and prototype with everything from hand tools to sophisticated CNC (computer numerical control) machines. Most makerspaces operate like community hobby shops where people gather to work on creative projects, often technical in nature, but also involving textiles, metalsmithing, automotive, scale modeling, and more.

Many hacker- and makerspaces are membership based, operating much like a health club, with various member levels allowing access to different tools and resources and are focused on independent craft,

repair, and construction. FabLabs, often associated with academic institutions or sponsored by a foundation or organization, tend to have a
manufacturing focus and a client base seeking business incubation
through rapid prototyping and knowledge development.

MAKERSPACES IN LIBRARIES

The first library-based makerspace, the Fayetteville Free Library Fab
Lab, opened in 2010 in Fayetteville, New York. In this case, Fab Lab
stands for "Fabulous Lab." It was developed by librarian Lauren Britton, who said in a *Library as Incubator* article in 2012, "Makerspaces
are places where people come together to create, collaborate, and share
resources and knowledge—an idea and concept that fits perfectly with
the mission and vision of public libraries."[4]

Fayetteville Free Library's Fab Lab first focused on 3D printers, still
a rare sight in 2010. Since then, the growth of creative public spaces in
libraries has been significant. A 2013 "Makerspaces in Libraries Survey," by John Burke, found that of 109 respondents, 41 percent were
already providing makerspaces or maker-style activities and programs in
their libraries. Another 36 percent had plans under way for makerspace
development in the near future.[5] Over 50 percent of the makerspaces
were in public libraries, with most of the rest in academic libraries and a
small percentage in public school libraries.

Today, the Fayetteville Library Fab Lab is just one of three distinct
makerspaces in the library. In addition to the fabrication resources
available at the Fab Lab, the library also has a Creation Lab for digital
exploration and a Little Makerspace for 5- to 8-year-olds. Besides 3D
printers, the library now boasts a PSP Super Computer, on loan, and
3D design programming, book making, and MakerBot sessions with a
librarian to learn the basics of digital fabrication and printing. And
Fayetteville is only one of dozens of library makerspaces across the
country putting fabrication and DIY creative capabilities into the hands
of ordinary citizens in communities nationwide.

DIFFERENT TYPES OF MAKERSPACES

Making is timeless and universal. Its current manifestation as a *maker movement*, a contemporary variation on the DIY movement, has been characterized by *Forbes* magazine as the new industrial revolution.[6] President Barack Obama, during the first ever White House Maker Faire, nominated the maker movement as one of the greatest opportunities for the American economy.[7] Makers can be found in numerous physical locations, roughly divided in hackerspaces, makerspaces, and FabLabs. These descriptions are often used interchangeably, but doing so disregards the distinctive signature and history of these different creative communities.

According to Nicholas Schiller, "Hackers are people who empower themselves with information in order to modify their environment and make the world a better place."

"There's no imperative," writes Schiller in "Hacker Values ≈ Library Values,"[8] "that hackers have to work with code, computers, or technology—although many do. Besides the traditional computer software hacker, there are many kinds of crafters, tinkerers, and makers that share the core hacker values. These makers all share knowledge about their world and engage in hands-on modification of it in order to make it a better place."

Walk into any makerspace and you see how people work together on a variety of projects across a range of scales. For instance, a number of international FabLabs are working on creating an inexpensive bamboo arm prosthesis. In another example, a Dutch mathematics teacher worked with Amsterdam FabLab to remedy the lack of the letter Pi in the traditional "chocoladeletter" holiday treat by making a silicone template for it.

Makerspaces are places where kids are playfully introduced to the operation of electronics or learning how to program. In colleges and universities, they are places where students can get more serious projects started. The World Bank is studying the growth of makerspaces and their impact on communities to see if they can be deployed in developing countries.[9]

What Are Hackerspaces, Makerspaces, and FabLabs?

The word "makerspace" is often used as an umbrella term for the different known descriptions of hackerspace, makerspace, or FabLab. Let's look at some of the distinguishing features of these different spaces for a better understanding of the original purpose and intent of each.

Hackerspaces

In the mid-1990s, hackerspaces emerged in Germany. These were places where computer programmers shared knowledge and infrastructure with each other. The well-known hackers conference Chaos Communication Camp brought the phenomenon to the attention of American hackers in 2007, which led to a growth of American hackerspaces. Unlike the German hackerspaces, American users weren't only concerned with programming and hacking, but they worked on physical projects as well. The development of the leading 3D printer from MakerBot Industries, which started in the New York hackerspace NYC Resistor, was one of the first products developed at a hackerspace.

Gui Cavalcanti, founder of Artisan's Asylum, a successful "community craft studio" located in Somerville, Massachusetts, described "hacking" succinctly in a 2013 article in *Make:* "There's a basic understanding that 'hacking' refers to a specific subset of activities that involve making existing objects do something unexpected."[10]

Makerspaces

Around 2005, makerspaces began to emerge. The concept became really popular with the publication of *Make:* magazine. The idea of a space for making offered a suitable way for initiatives that preferred not to associate with hackers, a label that had (and still has) a negative connotation. A makerspace is a kind of mini factory where objects are manufactured based on digital designs with 3D printers and CNC machines, and other types of more traditional equipment like lathes, as well as through more basic methods using textiles and other materials.

Conceptually, makerspaces differ quite a bit from hackerspaces, since makers are concerned with a wide range of crafts and don't focus exclusively on electronics and programming. Makerspaces often have an educational focus aimed at youth and families. Anyone can start a maker- or hackerspace: There are no special requirements or rules for the development of these creative spaces, just a like-minded community seeking space to build, invent, and tinker.

FabLabs

On the other side of the organizational spectrum are FabLabs. The FabLab, short for fabrication laboratory, was started by Neil Gershenfeld at the Center for Bits and Atoms in the Massachusetts Institute of Technology (MIT) Media Lab around 2005. Gershenfeld was inspired by the succes of his own MIT course called "How to Make (Almost) Anything." FabLabs are intended to be an open but structured creative community of fabricators, artists, scientists, engineers, educators, students, amateurs, and professionals of all ages. Typically operated by nonprofit organizations, there are now 448 FabLabs in 70 countries. [11]

Unlike maker- and hackerspaces, FabLabs are guided by a Fab Charter that outlines requirements that all FabLabs should have in common. All FabLabs, for instance, should start with the same basic set of tools and instruments. Additionally, all FabLabs must be open to the public during a portion of normal operating hours. FabLabs encourage entrepreneurship and self-motivation through informal learning environments and strive to produce measurable results through patent development or other productive efforts.

Of these different types of creative spaces, the one most compatible with libraries is the makerspace, though there is also a growing number of library FabLabs, especially in Europe.

RELATIONSHIP BETWEEN LIBRARIES AND MAKERSPACES

The history of makerspaces in libraries can be traced to the 2010 creation of the first public library makerspace, the Fayetteville Free Library Fab Lab, in Fayetteville, New York. The Fab Lab effort was a direct outgrowth of the maker movement, kicked off by the first Maker Faire in California in 2006.

Around that time, Lauren Britton, then a master of library and information sciences student at Syracuse, took a course called "Innovation and Public Libraries." It was there she first learned about 3D printing and became interested in trying to develop makerspaces in public libraries. The challenges of implementing in-house space use changes at any library at the time were considerable, so she came up with the idea of a mobile makerspace as more practical for other libraries to duplicate than a permanent building.

In a look back at Britton's effort, librarian Melody Clark observed, "This was a really huge stretch for the community to understand that the library was a place where they could create and make things—use a 3D printer, a laser cutter, a sewing machine. She worked to shift the perception of libraries as places where people consume things to the perception that the library could be a place to create."

More importantly, Britton found that "people who had never visited the library began streaming in."

Britton feels libraries and makerspaces belong together. "Libraries create an opening for people to experience the maker movement for free," she told Clark. "Libraries spend 69 percent of their budgets on print materials. Libraries should think of their collections in terms of the community members they serve—your collection is your community."[12]

LIBRARIES AS THE THIRD PLACE

Britton's comments echo the idea of the library as a "Third Place," a concept developed by Ray Oldenburg, PhD, author of *The Great Good Place*.[13]

"Nothing contributes so much to one's sense of belonging to a community as much as 'membership' in a third place," says Oldenburg, a professor emeritus of sociology at the University of West Florida in Pensacola. In 2014, his ideas about the Third Place were highlighted in a PBS series called Cool Spaces! The Best New Architecture that featured innovative library spaces.

Oldenburg proposed the concept of the Third Place in *The Great Good Place* as the place that isn't home and isn't work or school. The Third Place is that other space where we routinely meet up with friends and family to eat, talk, and companionably socialize. These "great good places," Oldenburg points out, are the neutral safe spaces that we voluntarily seek out and look forward to being in. We go there purely for the enjoyment of being together, without obligations, responsibilities, or concerns.

The Third Place is characterized as:

- a place outside of home or workplace,
- free or inexpensive,
- welcoming and comfortable,
- highly inclusive,
- usually having food, and
- intellectually and socially stimulating.

Pubs, cafés, bookstores and coffeehouses, and similar gathering places are the heart of community vitality, says Oldenburg, and the cornerstone of democracy. The Project for Public Spaces, a nonprofit planning, design, and educational organization dedicated to building stronger communities through accessible public spaces, notes such spaces "provide a setting for grassroots politics, create habits of public association, and offer psychological support to individuals and communities."

The Third Place is that vital "place on the corner" that helps unify neighborhoods, serves as ports of entry for newcomers to an area, provides intergenerational interaction, and enables discussion, entertainment, and friendship.

That sounds a whole lot like the local public library, especially like the public libraries that are working to revitalize themselves as active gathering places through makerspace development to become places where people can not only read, but also where they can talk, create, have fun, learn things, and generally have a good time together in a safe, inclusive environment.

The library as a Third Place isn't a new concept, of course. It was the driving motivator behind the design of many of the libraries featured in the Cool Spaces! library episode, and there have been several articles about the idea (see "School Library as Third Place"[14] and "Libraries, Coffeehouses and Third Places,"[15] for examples). But as libraries rebuild themselves in new ways, as makerspaces, with coffee shops and digital commons, with spaces for conversation, music, and more, the library card takes on new value as a membership card to every community's Third Place, and libraries take on new significance at the heart of our communities as places of action, as well as of thought.

NOTES

1. Cristina Benton, Lori Mullins, Kristin Shelley, and Tim Dempsey, *Makerspaces: Supporting an Entrepreneurial System*, working paper, Michigan State University, 2013, http://www.reicenter.org/upload/documents/colearning/benton2013_report.pdf.

2. "Setting Up a Makerspace," HubPages, June 3, 2014, http://cosmosscience.hubpages.com/hub/Setting-up-a-Makerspace (accessed October 10, 2014).

3. "About Maker Faire: A Bit of History," Maker Faire, http://makerfaire.com/makerfairehistory (accessed October 10, 2014).

4. "The Oh-So Fabulous Lab at the Fayetteville Free Library," The Library as Incubator Project, March 21, 2012, http://www.libraryasincubatorproject.org/?p=3335 (accessed October 10, 2014).

5. Gary Price, "Results from 'Makerspaces in Libraries' Study Released," LJ INFOdocket, December 16, 2013, http://www.infodocket.com/2013/12/16/results-of-makerspaces-in-libraries-study-released (accessed October 10, 2014).

6. Dan Schwabel, "Chris Anderson: How the Makers Will Create a New Industrial Revolution," *Forbes*, October 4, 2012.

7. "FACT SHEET: President Obama to Host First-Ever White House Maker Faire," The White House, June 18, 2014, http://www.whitehouse.gov/the-press-office/2014/06/18/fact-sheet-president-obama-host-first-ever-white-house-maker-faire (accessed November 14, 2014).

8. Nicholas Schiller, "Hacker Values ≈ Library Values," ACRL TechConnect Blog, November 13, 2012, http://acrl.ala.org/techconnect/?p=2282 (accessed November 14, 2014).

9. *Crowdfunding's Potential for the Developing World*. Washington, DC: World Bank, infoDev, Finance and Private Sector Development Department, 2013.

10. Gui Cavalcanti, "Is It a Hackerspace, Makerspace, TechShop, or FabLab?" *Make:*, May 22, 2013.

11. "Labs | FabLabs," FabLabs.io, https://www.fablabs.io/labs (accessed January 11, 2015).

12. Melody Clark, "Libraries & Makerspaces: A Revolution?" Technology and Social Change Group, June 13, 2014, http://tascha.uw.edu/2014/06/libraries-makerspaces-a-revolution/ (accessed September 11, 2014).

13. Ray Oldenburg, *The Great Good Place: Cafés, Coffee Shops, Community Centers, Beauty Parlors, General Stores, Bars, Hangouts, and How They Get You through the Day* (New York: Paragon House, 1989).

14. Mark Ray, "School Library as Third Place," Librarian-Provocateur, https://librarian-provocateur.wikispaces.com/School Library as Third Place (accessed September 11, 2014).

15. Melanie A. Lyttle and Shawn D. Walsh. "Libraries, Coffeehouses, and Third Places," Public Libraries Online, November 15, 2013, http://publiclibrariesonline.org/2013/11/libraries-coffeehouses-and-third-places/ (accessed September 11, 2014).

2

GETTING STARTED WITH MAKERSPACES

THE LIBRARY OF THE FUTURE

Google "Library of the Future" and you get 350 million results. Many examinations of the twenty-first-century library include comments like "this isn't your childhood library" or "no longer a warehouse for barely touched tomes," remarks that can feel threatening as much as they can sound promising.

A lot of us liked our childhood libraries, and we touched as many tomes as we could—and still do! We like having quiet, safe places to go and be alone with our thoughts and imaginations, to travel the world on a library card. But the facts of the matter demand action to keep libraries both a sanctuary for book lovers and a meaningful part of our communities for people who might benefit from new functionality from our public libraries.

Library and Community Assessment

A recent Pew Research study on libraries found that while most people know where their local library is and 97 percent of Americans highly value their libraries, only 30 percent can be classified as "high engagement" users, with another 40 percent classified as "medium engagement" for having "used a library in the past year."[1] The remaining 30 percent are fairly disengaged from their public libraries. Changing up library offerings and—perhaps more to the point—reimagining the library is a natural next step toward reengaging the public with these vital centers of community.

In a related Pew study called "Library Services in the Digital Age," researchers noted that "many librarians said they were intrigued by the idea of makerspaces, or workshops where patrons can work on hands-on projects and collaborations. Similarly, several library staff members said they wished their library could offer digitization resources for local history materials, professional-grade office services such as videoconferencing, as well as renovated spaces that would encourage collaboration and allow the library to offer more types of services."[2]

And that, in fact, is where many libraries are now headed, looking at ways to revitalize programs and repurpose space to better serve communities and provide new avenues of enjoyment and fulfillment for all users, rebuilding their programs in the service of becoming exciting and relevant hubs of community engagement. Makerspaces in libraries, or their close cousins, digital commons or innovation centers, are making some of the biggest headlines, from Westport, Connecticut, to Missoula, Montana, from Chicago to Tampa, Florida.

Success = Collaborative and Community Driven

Some efforts to create the "Library of the Future" will falter and fall short. Those will often be the result of forced innovation driven from the top down, reflecting administrative and marketing visions of what constitutes "the future."

Others will totally flip what people think of libraries and will bring excitement, energy, and endless possibilities to our communities, helping move us toward that necessary culture of active creation from one of passive consumption.

The libraries that succeed with their twenty-first-century makeovers will be those that are community driven, as much about programming that reflects community needs and interests as they are about space use. These types of programming reflect a necessarily fearless approach to reimagining what a public library is, expanding from a static collection of archival knowledge to an active content and program delivery system.

Identifying Stakeholders

The only way to really know what a community wants and feels it needs from its library is to ask. There are typically three groups of stakeholders whose views about library programming and development are vital to successful implementation:

1. patrons: youth and adults
2. library staff and volunteers
3. general community

Adult patrons and youth patrons are separated for good reason: These groups tend to use libraries differently and may have vastly different notions of what constitutes "usefulness," so it's important to assess each group individually if possible. Understanding library staff and volunteer native interests can help with the creation of programs that staff and volunteers enjoy providing, thereby enhancing the experience for patrons as well, because passionate learning guides provide the most fulfilling experience for both learners and teachers.

And having a good understanding of the immediate library neighborhood or community can help your library connect with potential content delivery and program development partners who already possess the skills and resources needed to create powerful programs. Leveraging partners with existing expertise provides a ready, cost-effective (free!) professional volunteer base to complement library staffing resources.

Discovery Sessions through Community Conversations

It's fairly easy to identify patrons, both young and older, and of course you already know your library staff and volunteers. Identifying your immediate community stakeholders can take a little sleuthing though. You can start by mining meeting records: What groups meet or have met at your library? Who has held special programs or events?

You can expand that search through Google Maps, by searching "nearby" your location, on terms like "engineering," "education," "electronics," "sewing," "hobby clubs," "woodworking," "professional associations," and similar phrases related to the types of groups you think might be interested in creative programming at your library.

Makerspace Design Plan   John F. Germany Public Library

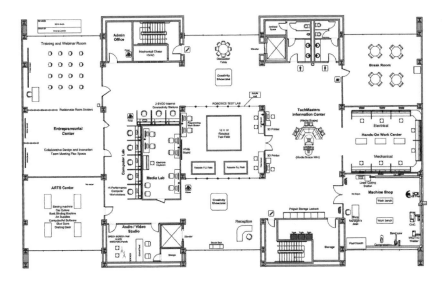

Developed by Steve & Terri Willingham, Willingham Associates, LLC for the John F. Germany Library

HIVE Floor Plan

Invite each group: youth patrons, adult patrons, volunteers and staff, and community stakeholders to their own open house or community conversation event. Serve refreshments and light snacks and open the floor. You might do a short presentation on makerspaces in libraries and let guests know how important their views are to creating the type of library programming and functionality that best serves their needs, and then field questions and ideas.

For younger patrons like a teen advisory board, a more effective discovery session might center on a gaming night or hands-on activities, encouraging more free-flow discussion when hands and minds are engaged. Perhaps have on hand a variety of projects and resources that might be made available through new programming to see what younger patrons are naturally drawn to or where interests arise.

For library staff and volunteers, consider hosting a "build night" with some activity led by individuals with expertise in a particular area, and invite attendees to share their ideas about their hobbies and interests.

Willingham
Associates

Land O'Lakes Branch Library
Creative Spaces Conceptual Layout
Recommended Space Plan

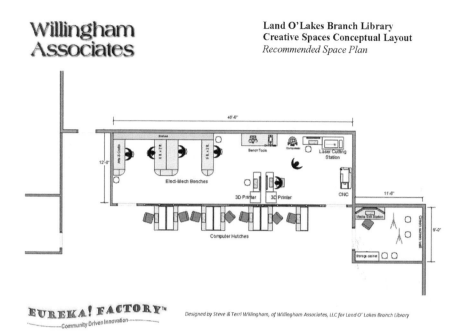

EUREKA! FACTORY™   *Designed by Steve & Terri Willingham, of Willingham Associates, LLC for Land O' Lakes Branch Library*
-------Community Driven Innovation-------

Land O' Lakes (Florida) Library Floor Plan

Look for trends—gaming, sewing, woodworking, model building, etc.—and consider ways to integrate those existing interests into library programming. People who have an opportunity to share what they love will be enjoyable to be with and inspire greater engagement among patrons and greater buy-in by other stakeholders, like administration and government agencies.

For community stakeholders, consider a more sophisticated gathering, with hors d'oeuvres and perhaps a presentation by a local business leader. This is an opportunity to highlight the economic development aspect of enhancing library services with creative programming. Invite brainstorming from business and community leaders about ways they might like to see library programming expanded or developed, and then invite them to be part of making their ideas happen.

Document and Follow Up

Take the results of your discovery sessions and map them out, both ideologically and geographically. Look for trends in hobby or business opportunities and strong interest among individuals or groups and use this information as the foundations of your makerspace and creative programming efforts. And follow up with participants with invitations to additional sessions, trial programs, offers of teaching space, or opportunities to share more information or ideas. It's important to nurture interest and not let it languish after you've invited input.

The true "Library of the Future" will be collaborative and community driven. It will remain a cherished institution, with quiet places to read and think and vicariously journey, as well as active spaces and programming for academic and workforce skills development and personal fulfillment. It will contribute to economic development and generate pride of ownership and commensurately increased relevancy and vibrancy in the community.

DEVELOPING A MAKERSPACE PLAN AND BUDGET

Planning for creative space use in any library will necessarily require a tailored approach that meets the unique needs and addresses the specific challenges of each library. Designs should be flexible and adaptable to the needs and preferences of a library and its staff and patrons and should be considered a dynamic process. The best makerspace plans will allow for spaces that can be rearranged, removed, expanded or reduced, or repurposed as time and circumstances dictate.

Makerspace designs should take into consideration the results of community, staff, and volunteer discovery sessions, as well as a comprehensive review of existing building infrastructure, capabilities, and community demographics and extensive research into existing makerspaces and other similar creative and cowork spaces that might be in the area. Combining the results of in-person discovery sessions with facilities inventory and planning with an eye to future agility will provide the best chances for long-term success of any library makerspace effort.

Space Allocation

Libraries necessarily vary in physical size, scope of services, and staffing, but there are some basic rules of thumb that can be taken into consideration for almost any size library interested in developing almost any size creative space. These include:

- Emergency Aisles: As generally recommended by most fire codes, 25 to 35 percent of floor space should be open, with clear egress to emergency exits.
- Direct Access: All rooms and work spaces should ideally be accessed directly from common traffic areas without the need to pass through other rooms and spaces.
- Classroom and Conference/Coworking Space: For maximum comfort and productivity, allow 20 to 50 square feet per seated person in work spaces.
- Physical Work Space: Workshop areas should allow 75 to 100 square feet of independent work space per person so that people don't get in each other's way.

Scope and Design

Based on the results of discovery sessions and facilities reviews, you should have a pretty solid idea of whether your library is in a position to develop some sort of physical makerspace or if you'll be focusing on creative maker-style programming instead or some combination of both. Libraries that are truly pressed for space and can't find a square inch to repurpose may often still be able allocate a desktop or two for a 3D printer or put a sewing machine in a meeting room for weekly textiles work.

Another option is pop-up maker programming, quite literally a makerspace-in-a-box that utilizes a variety of tools and resources, ranging from SparkFun kits and Arduinos to soldering kits and hand tools that are kept stored but easily accessible for special programs and events. Pop-up programming provides an engaging way to introduce patrons to creative ways of enjoying the library, familiarizing the library community about maker culture and opportunities in a way that puts little to no strain on space constraints.

For libraries with a little space to spare, and even with a lot, space designs should reflect community needs and interests. You don't want to invest in 3D printers when patrons are more interested in graphic design or woodworking, and vice versa. And mileage will vary on final designs, as actual usage determines what works and what doesn't. Best to heed the words of Ralph Waldo Emerson, who said, "A foolish consistency is the hobgoblin of little minds," and plan accordingly. It will probably take at least a year before a new space settles into its most useful groove.

Budgeting

With that in mind, it's best to build out in phases and to budget responsibly. Creativity can and should be applied in selecting the most useful, affordable, or practical options for library makerspaces. Substitutions and adaptations can always be made, especially in the case of software and many media tools. It may be tempting to run and buy one of everything, but resist that temptation.

It's possible to create a highly enjoyable low-budget space with locally sourced and in-kind donations, and with creative planning it's also possible to create a well-stocked, high-tech facility. Some key things to consider in developing a budget:

- Staffing: Will you have dedicated staff or will you be able to utilize volunteer expertise and support? Community discovery sessions can be key to providing volunteer support and reducing impact on staff.
- Equipment: A basic 3D printer will run about $1,500, but you could also make your own for about $500 with some volunteers and dedicated staff and then 3D print additional printers as needed. That's the glory of a makerspace—with well-placed community support, you can essentially build, source, and secure through in-kind donations much of the equipment that you may need or want. Again, building out in phases allows for the gradual acquisition and identification of necessary equipment in a fiscally responsible manner.
- Remodeling: If you can fit space development into existing facilities, costs are commensurately reduced. But take into considera-

tion things like portable walls to create space within space, electrical drops, repainting walls with whiteboard paint, improved lighting, installing outside ventilation if you're looking at any kind of cutting machinery, and any additional furnishings that may be required.

- Consumable supplies that need to be regularly restocked can include 3D printer filament, solder wire, art and office supplies, and sewing supplies.
- Maintenance: A core volunteer staff can help supervise space use and provide regular maintenance checks and repairs as needed, but if you have any kind of machinery in your space, it will require evaluations of mechanical and tool conditions, cleaning and oiling of any large tools and power equipment, and ventilation inspection.
- Software License Renewal: Software license seats will need to be renewed annually or every few years, depending on software packages, and will have associated costs.

Potential Funding Sources

Like any library project, there are a variety of ways to potentially fund makerspaces and creative programming, ranging from Institute of Museum and Library Services (IMLS) grants[3] to your friends group to community investors. Don't overlook the power of naming rights either. A common practice in most libraries for meeting rooms and special areas, offering naming rights to your makerspace, or portions of it, can be a resourceful and community-building way to help fund your space. That's certainly the case for the Hazel L. Incantalupo MakerSpace at Palm Harbor Library in Florida, an innovative arts-focused children's makerspace funded in large part through a multiyear naming rights option.[4]

DEVELOPING A MAKERSPACE HANDBOOK AND OTHER FOUNDING DOCUMENTS

As critical as identifying stakeholders and their needs and interests to drive the success and patron engagement of your library makerspace is the documentation that will give it longevity and make it reproducible in other libraries. For any good journey, you need a map; for any good business, you need a plan. A makerspace is in the business of taking people on creative journeys, so you need to document accordingly with a good management plan and a sufficiently adaptable map to help you move forward.

Useful documentation for your individual library makerspace will vary according to the size, contents, intent, and actual use of your space. If you have a lot of hand or power tools, you'll need documentation about tool use protocol, orientation, shop management, safety, and required releases. If your space provides mostly creative programming with passive resources like art supplies or computers, then your documentation will reflect that reality.

The most adaptable format for almost any type of library makerspace will be a dynamic Makerspace Handbook that codifies all the necessary legal, practical, and historical documentation; space use policies; Code of Conduct; and any other protocols unique to your library culture and programming.

The Essentials

Your table of contents should include:

- Welcome: A short welcome letter from library administration, with a description of your space and its mission and goals.
- History: May include bylaws, if separately organized, and mission and vision statements.
- Makerspace Policy and Rules
- Member/Patron Agreements

Most of these are self-explanatory but we'll explore a few sections in a little greater detail.

Makerspace Policy and Rules

There are many sample makerspace policies available, but the best policy is the one that meets the needs of your library with respect to facilities staff and program support, and matches your library's goals with the allotted space. Having a basic mission or statement of purpose can provide the framework around which to develop useful policies. Is the space intended to serve mostly children? Is it arts focused? Does it support skills training? Is it mostly for prototyping?

The community assessment sessions with patrons and staff can help answer these questions and others about space use and focus. Once you've identified the mission of the space, then you can start fleshing out the details. The Makerspace Policy and Rules section should include information about:

- Hours of Operation: Is the space open during library hours or only on special days and times?
- Membership: Who can use the space, and under what conditions and terms of service? What ages? Are guardians required for children of a certain age? Is usage limited to members with library cards?
- Library Policy and Rules: Make sure space policies are in alignment with library policies.
- Code of Conduct: Advocates for Youth has a "Safe Spaces" statement that lends itself well to library makerspaces. What are the consequences of not adhering to the Code of Conduct?
- Scheduling Policy: How will space use be scheduled, and how long can spaces be used?
- Safety Rules: Will orientation be required before some or all equipment may be used? Do patrons need to supply their own safety gear, like safety glasses, or will the library? What types of creative activities are permitted and which are prohibited?
- Housekeeping and Maintenance: Quite literally, who cleans up and maintains equipment—library staff or space users? Regular "town halls" can be useful to institute in makerspaces, providing an opportunity for active makerspace users to take some ownership over the facility and lessening the work of staff.
- Guest Policy: Are outside guests permitted? How many? How often? Are library cards required of guests or only of members?

Member Agreements

Each space makes its own policies and decides how to enforce them, and member agreements may or may not be in order depending on library organizational structure and space use intentions. However, it's not a bad idea to have some agreements in place for future if not immediate use, and if only to articulate expectations of patrons and staff regarding space use. Standard member agreements that are good to include in a handbook are:

- Member Agreement: outlining expectations about meetings, guests, access, and cleanup.
- Member Consent and Release Form: covering publicity and marketing; the use of participant photos in brochures, websites, and social media; the use of personal equipment; and safety agreements attesting that the user has read and is informed about safety policies.
- Hold Harmless Agreement: a basic boilerplate or customized document, waiving (at least in theory) any library liability in case of personal injury or the loss or destruction of items made in the makerspace.
- Guest Release Form: if guests will be permitted, outlining expectations and responsibilities.

This document, like your makerspace design itself, should be dynamic, fluid, and regularly revisited. As your space grows, adapts, and changes, your Makerspace Handbook should reflect those changes as well. The document should be easily available and accessible on site, as well as online, and every space user should be provided with a digital copy of the handbook.

Expectations and responsibilities are the heart of a Makerspace Handbook, leaving as little to chance as possible with respect to space, tool, equipment usage, and conduct. Additionally, having a Makerspace Handbook shows intentionality and a long-term commitment to safety, transparency, and quality management, setting a tone of maturity, professionalism, and respect across the board.

Codifying policy and member use protocols also ensures continuity and makes it easier for volunteers and staff down the road to continue managing a space and provides a reliable guide for those who come after, both as patrons and staff, to continue using your library maker-space safely and productively for many years to come.

PROVIDING HANDS-ON TRAINING

In Europe, FabLabs are a more common way to provide creative space in libraries. With the modular package *Fab the Library!* Bibliotheekser-vice Fryslân (Library Service Fryslân) helps other library organizations set up a library FabLab or makerspace. In Europe, it's the first library organization to establish a FabLab, called FryskLab.[5] The modular package came about thanks to support from the Netherlands Institute for Public Libraries (SIOB). The program is built upon the notion that the inclusion of a FabLab in a library gives new impetus to the library by stimulating innovation and (local) economic activity without aban-doning its core library values.

Fab the Library! has a number of objectives, including the develop-ment of twenty-first-century skills for libraries, librarians, and visitors; inspiring the development of new crafts and craftmanship, entrepen-eurship, and creativity; and creating new opportunities for youth. *Fab the Library!* also encourages the sharing of knowledge and information and new ways to integrate emerging technologies in library services and making them available to the public.

Fab the Library! currently only serves Dutch libraries, but the ob-jective is to make it an international program. *Fab the Library!* consists of three modules:

- Module 1, Introduction: FabLab: "How to Make Almost Any-thing" (duration: 4 hours)
- Module 2, Practice: The Machines: 101 course on digital fabrica-tion (duration: 4 hours)
- Module 3, Strategy: Implementing FabLab (duration: 4 hours)

The first module utilizes presentation and interactive demos to intro-duce library staff to the concept of FabLab, its history and underlying principles, digital fabrication, and the principles of open design. The second one gives library staff firsthand experience in using the various FabLab equipment, which is traditionally more machine-intensive than a makerspace. The standard machines in a FabLab consist of a laser cutter, a 3D printer, a vinyl cutter, an embroidery machine, and a milling machine.

In the third module, participants learn about different business models of FabLabs and design a solid funding/revenue model for their own situation. Here, all services of the FabLab community are introduced: workshops, training, guidance, and the Fab Academy program, which provides advanced digital fabrication instruction for FabLab users.[6] Furthermore, the political and economic landscape around Fab-Labs is explored, with a focus on the technical conditions that each FabLab must meet.

This type of robust, hands-on training helps librarians instituting FabLabs in their facilities get a well-rounded look at what's involved and how to structure services for patrons around this new type of active librarianship.

HOW TO REALIZE A SUSTAINABLE MAKERSPACE/ FABLAB IN YOUR LIBRARY

The *Fab the Library!* training program serves as a solid introduction to makerspaces and FabLabs in libraries for everyone from staff and volunteers to administrators. But the biggest challenge for any FabLab or makerspace is achieving a sustainable business model. To that end, it's important to understand what activities ensure that the makerspace or FabLab won't dissolve after a short time.

The general experience is that many Labs often quite easily get a starting budget or initial funding but lack long-term planning for sustainability. John Boeck and Peter Troxler conducted a FabLab Business Study in 2011, which resulted in eight identifiable business models for FabLabs.[7] In an interview for the *Fab the Library!* program, Troxler said he believes three are the most suitable for libraries[8]:

- grant-based, with a main income stream from public or private funding;
- embedded in educational institutions, with no main income stream but where expenses are covered and services are provided by the parent institution;

- educational activities model, with the main income stream generated from course and workshop fees and services typically approved or accredited and led by FabLab instructors.

The other models aren't particularly relevant to libraries, but can be explored in their entirety at the FabLab Iceland Wiki page: http://wiki.fablab.is.

All labs in Troxler's study indicated their main business model was providing access to infrastructure that users would have no access to otherwise. Most of them also indicated that providing access to knowledge of the FabLab network and giving access to experts were equally part of their value. Troxler believes that there are two possible value propositions, namely FabLabs providing facilities and FabLabs providing innovation support.[9]

We'll take a closer look at each of the three business models Troxler recommends for libraries interested in developing sustainable makerspaces or FabLabs.

Grant-Based

This option requires that there always must be manpower to write funding proposals. This requires an understanding of the possibilities and identification of funding and business opportunities. Given the attention that currently exists for maker culture, this is a promising way to get financial support. The disadvantage is that many funds do not provide structural operational support. This means that there must be a sequence of activities to make the lab remain active and visible for the general public.

Some recommendations:

- Take time to gather knowledge of funding and sponsorship opportunities.
- Some entrepreneurial skills are essential.
- Continuous development of project proposals is necessary.

Institutionally Embedded

The phenomenon of a FabLab within an existing organization is obvious for library makerspaces. In contrast to "independent" laboratories, this has the benefit that staffing is often already provided since the library has dedicated staff, though the library may have to invest in focused training to get existing staff up to speed to be able to work in a lab setting. Since the budget of labs is mainly spent on the long-term labor costs, this can be a great advantage for libraries. This also goes for the cost of housing. In conjunction with applying for project grants, this is a promising model for libraries.

Recommendations:

- Approach employees that are known to be willing to work in the library lab.
- Be prepared to find colleagues whom you might not expect to be willing and able to contribute.
- Make the lab an essential part of business operations and try to find as much support as possible within the organization.

Educational Activities

Labs in libraries almost always have a strong educational component. Media literacy, for example, can be linked perfectly to elements of maker culture, like alternative copyright models (Creative Commons). This model, however, requires time spent on the development of educational materials. The reimbursement of related costs could come from a project subsidy. Participants in activities can also be asked for a financial contribution through course fees or donation requests. In addition, a lasting relationship with educational institutions can be built.

Recommendations:

- Think of good ideas for your educational offering that is distinctive from other providers.
- Work on a good lasting cooperation with educational and other community partners.
- Leverage public school use of lab facilities.

Depending on the type of library and the desire of the user, other choices are obviously possible. Ultimately, each local situation determines the best model for each library based on an understanding of library capabilities and resources, staff and stakeholder interests and abilities, and community needs and preferences.

NOTES

1. Kathryn Zickuhr, Kristen Purcell, and Lee Rainie, "From Distant Admirers to Library Lovers—and Beyond," Pew Research Internet Project, March 13, 2014, http://www.pewinternet.org/2014/03/13/library-engagement-typology/ (accessed August 28, 2014).

2. Kathryn Zickuhr, Lee Rainie, and Kristen Purcell, "Library Services in the Digital Age," Pew Research Internet Project, January 22, 2013, http://libraries.pewinternet.org/2013/01/22/library-services (accessed August 28, 2014).

3. Institute of Museum and Library Services, http://www.imls.gov (accessed October 20, 2014).

4. Linda Bragg, "Grand Opening of Palm Harbor Library's Hazel L. Incantalupo MakerSpace," Palm Harbor Patch, July 12, 2014, http://patch.com/florida/palmharbor/grand-opening-of-palm-harbor-librarys-hazel-l-incantalupo-makerspace.

5. John Burke, "An Overview of Makerspace Implementations," in *Makerspaces: A Practical Guide for Librarians* (Lanham, MD: Rowman & Littlefield, 2014), chapter 3.

6. "Fab Academy 2015," Fab Academy, http://www.fabacademy.org (accessed December 6, 2014).

7. John Boeck and Peter Troxler, "Sustainable Fab Labs," Fab Wiki, August 17, 2011, http://wiki.fablab.is/images/e/ef/Factsheet_LabSustainability_Fab7.pdf (accessed December 4, 2014).

8. "Business Patterns," Fab Wiki, October 12, 2012, http://wiki.fablab.is/wiki/Business_Patterns (accessed December 4, 2014).

9. "Business Models for Fab Labs," Openp2pdesignorg, http://www.openp2pdesign.org/projects/report-business-models-for-open-hardware-fab-labs-diy-craft/business-models-for-fab-labs/ (accessed December 4, 2014).

<h1 style="text-align:center">3</h1>

TOOLS AND APPLICATIONS

Working in a library makerspace obviously requires knowledge of a variety of tools and software. Fortunately, there is a lot of information, often made available online for free. In this chapter, we'll look at some of the most popular tools for 3D printing, laser cutting, electronics, and other makerspace resources. We'll also provide insight into a number of online sources of information on makerspaces and the things that can be made in them.

3D PRINTING

A 3D printer doesn't do anything without instructions for a design. These can be created with the use of modeling software or objects can be found in online repositories already configured for 3D printers. The third possibility is to make a 3D scan, which functions as a base object.

Design Software

There are a variety of 3D printing design software resources, ranging from software tools simple enough for children to use, like Tinkercad, to more sophisticated tools for advanced users. Some of the most popular include:

- Tinkercad, a 3D design tool: http://www.tinkercad.com

- Sculptris, a 3D sculpting tool: http://pixologic.com/sculptris
- SketchUp Make 3D, a design tool: http://www.sketchup.com
- Doodle3D, 2D design tool, especially for the 3D printer: http://www.doodle3d.com
- Blender 3D, design tool: http://www.blender.org/

Slicing Software

Most 3D models are not immediately suitable for 3D printing. An additional step called "slicing" is often required. Slicing programs provide the physical instructions from which the printer renders an object. Most printers utilize G-code files. Some printer manufacturers provide their own slicing software, but there independent alternatives, as well.

Some commonly used slicing software includes:

- Slicer: http://slicer.org/
- Cura: https://www.ultimaker.com/pages/our-software

3D Printers

A widely used source for finding information about 3D printers is the annual *Ultimate Guide to 3D Printing* by *Make:* magazine. Besides featuring well-known brands like MakerBot and Ultimaker, it also gives quite a lot of attention to small manufacturers and popular trends in 3D printing. In the most recent 2014 edition of the magazine, printers made by MakerBot, Ultimaker, and Up are best of class.

If your library does not have printers available but offers the facilities to create designs, printing can also be outsourced. Some resources for this purpose are:

- Shapeways: http://shapeways.com
- iMaterialise: http://i.materialise.com

3D Printers for Libraries

If a library has a makerspace, the 3D printer is usually part of it. For libraries, there are three main considerations:

1. The printer should work reliably.
2. The software should be easy to operate.
3. The printer must be easy to maintain.

With these requirements in mind, there are some good candidates for libraries.

Ultimaker 2

The Ultimaker 2 is used in a lot of FabLabs and makerspaces. Both the software and hardware are available as open source. However, this does not mean that it is a machine only of interest to tweakers and tinkerers. The Ultimaker 2 prints very accurately with both PLA (soft plastic) and ABS (hard plastic) and uses the proprietary Cura software. The machine is operated via Linux, Mac, and Windows and can also print from an SD card.

MakerBot Replicator 2

Like the Ultimaker 2, the Replicator 2 is used by both beginners and professionals. The Replicator 2 prints in PLA only and does it very well. Besides compatibility with Linux, Mac, and Windows, printing from an SD card is also supported. The MakerWare software is developed by MakerBot and is considered very user-friendly. The Replicator 2 is completely closed source.

Up Plus

Chinese printer Up Plus is used a lot in educational environments. It is a small and light device but has very good printing properties. It prints with PLA and ABS. Unlike Ultimaker and MakerBot, Linux is not supported, but printing from an SD card is. The function to calibrate the print bed automatically is very nice. The Up Plus hardware and software are closed source.

3D Scanning

Besides making your own design or using an existing one (see the repositories), 3D scanning is also an opportunity to create an object. A popular 3D scanner is the MakerBot Digitizer: http://store.makerbot.com/digitizer.

3D scanning is also possible by using multiple cameras. The available images must then be reworked into a printable file. An example of sofware that is capable of doing this is 123D Catch: http://www.123dapp.com/catch.

It is also possible to create a scan with Micrososoft Kinect. To make a printable object, you can make use of Scenect software (http://www.faro.com/scenect/scenect) and create something of truly remarkable proportions like a Scanotron 3D body scanner, from which you can produce mini-mes of yourself and friends.[1]

Repositories

There are a number of ways to find 3D designs online. These are often free to download or reuse. Some popular sites:

- Thingiverse and Youmagine—both with many printable (.STL) files. Thingiverse (http://www.thingiverse.com) is owned by MakerBot; Youmagine (http://www.youmagine.com) is owned by Ultimaker.
- SketchUp 3D Warehouse contains a range of designs created in SketchUp: http://3dwarehouse.sketchup.com.
- Instructables.com (http://www.instructables.com/id/3D-Printing-1/) is a site with a wide array of maker projects, including 3D printing. The site is owned by Autodesk and includes an introduction to 3D printing as well.
- A specific repository for 3D design programs that are created by applications offered by Autodesk is 123DAPP: http://www.123dapp.com/Gallery/content/all.
- On the EduTech Wiki, you can find a guide for teaching, but it is also excellent for libraries that are interested in digital fabrication: http://edutechwiki.unige.ch/en/3D_printers_in_education.

General news about 3D printing can be found on 3D Printing Industry: http://3dprintingindustry.com/ and 3Ders http://www.3ders.org/.

LASER CUTTING

The laser cutter uses a high-power laser beam to carve a two-dimensional path onto some type of material via cutting instructions generated by a computer. This makes it possible to either cut or engrave certain materials with very little waste. The result is a bladeless engraving and cutting tool with virtually limitless applications.

While 3D printers are en vogue, the laser cutter is the real workhorse of a FabLab. Though they look similar, there are two basic types of laser cutters: those with glass laser tubes and those with long-life metal RF (radio frequency) laser tubes. Glass tubes have a life span of around one thousand hours, while RF tubes can last for ten thousand hours. A replacement glass tube may cost $400, a replacement RF tube $4,000 dollars.

So the choice boils down to intended use and budget. Businesses that depend on a laser cutter typically utilize an RF-type machine, which can run as much as $35,000. Less heavy loads can be handled by a glass-tube laser cutter. Don't try to cut costs by ordering knockoff equipment direct from China. Order from a reputable company for a good, reliable machine.

Here are a few examples for glass-tube machines in use at FabLabs:

- HPC Laser for a A4 size machine: http://hpclaser.co.uk
- Full Spectrum Laser for a 50x30 machine: http://fslaser.com/products/lasers/hobby-lasers/newhobby
- BRM Laser for 40x60 to 90x125 machine: http://www.brmlasers.nl/prijzen-brm-lasermachine

And here are some examples with RF tubes:

- Epilog: https://www.epiloglaser.com
- Trotec: http://www.troteclaser.com/en-US/Pages/Laser_systems.aspx
- Laser Pro: http://www.laserprouk.com/

All six machines have satisfied users. But not all have software easy to use for users in a FabLab or a library. For instance, the job control language for Trotec lasers is relatively hard to handle. For a small library the FS Laser would be a good choice as you just hit ctrl-P and it cuts. This is also the type of laser used in the section "How to Create a Simple Laser-Cut Object" in chapter 5.

Beyond the type of laser tube used, the next consideration is the size of the cutting table that your facility can accommodate and the need for outside ventilation or a closed HEPA-filter system.

Tip: Laser cutting takes time. In many FabLabs you see people queuing up in front of the cutter waiting for their turn. That is not a bad thing, as they start talking to each other and teach each other how to shorten their waiting and cutting time and it provides some effective learning time. But most labs limit cutting time to fifteen to twenty minutes during free access periods.

A great source of information on laser cutters is provided by Adafruit. On their website (http://www.adafruit.com), they provide a wealth of information about laser cutters, including guidance on specific alignment of the lasers for different materials and purposes. It specifically discusses the Epilog laser cutter, which is included in the standard MIT inventory of FabLabs.[2] Another good resource is MiniFabLab, which provides a lot of information on laser cutters for smaller labs, which can be very helpful for libraries.[3]

Common design tools for laser cutters are often conventional 2D programs:

- Inkscape, open-source 2D design tool: http://inkscape.org
- CorelDraw and Adobe Illustrator, commercial 2D design tools: http://www.coreldraw.com/ and https://www.adobe.com/products/illustrator/

Although these common tools work perfectly fine with a laser cutter, they lack the mechanical drawing tools found with conventional computer-aided design (CAD) software. CAD is specifically tailored to produce working drawings by means of tools that really make prototyping and exporting to the laser cutter an easy thing to do. Two examples of CAD software:

- Draftsight: http://www.3ds.com/products/draftsight
- LibreCAD: http://librecad.org/cms/home.html

PROGRAMMING, ROBOTICS, AND ELECTRONICS

Besides 3D printing, many labs also focus on programming, robotics, and electronics. It is popular to work with Arduino, Raspberry Pi, Makey Makey, and littleBits. An object-oriented programming tool such as Scratch is often used to tinker and to teach programming to children. Here are some sources of information:

Arduino

The official website of Arduino, an open-source electronics platform with easy-to-use hardware and software, is at http://www.arduino.cc/. *Make:* magazine fills a blog with all kinds of information about Arduino. You'll find articles, projects, videos, and blogs: http://blog.makezine. com/arduino/. *Getting Started with Arduino* is an excellent book by Massimo Banzi.

Raspberry Pi

Raspberry Pi Foundation is the go-to spot on the web for all things Raspberry Pi: http://www.raspberrypi.org/. Raspberry Pi is the colorful name of a tiny library-card-sized programmable computer that can be used for a variety of projects. *Make:* magazine has a substantial Raspberry Pi library on their website at http://blog.makezine.com/category/electronics/raspberry-pi/.

Programming

Scratch is a free programming language with a graphic interface to create simple storytelling and games. The website contains materials and videos for educators and classrooms: http://scratch.mit.edu/.

Hardware Kits

MaKey MaKey (http://www.makeymakey.com/) is an "invention kit for everyone." It creates a simple alligator-clip-based interface between a computer and everyday objects, like a banana. It plugs into the USB port of any computer, even a Raspberry Pi, and turns household objects into a keyboard or joystick. Similar kits include:

- Drawdio allows you to turn a pencil into a simple music synthesizer. You can play music while you write! http://web.media.mit.edu/~silver/drawdio/.
- littleBits uses modules that snap together with magnets to learn about and prototype with electronics: http://littlebits.cc/.
- BARE Conductive Touch Board is designed to turn almost any material or surface into a sensor: http://www.bareconductive.com/.

OPEN DESIGN, OPEN DATA, AND OPEN SOURCE

Open Design Now is a production of Premsela Netherlands Institute for Design and Fashion, Waag Society, and Creative Commons Netherlands in association with BIS Publishers. The book contains great articles about open design and is freely available: http://opendesignnow.org/.

FACILITATING PEER PRODUCTION AND SHARING

Key elements of the maker movement are sharing and collaboration. Beyond the physical environment of the makerspace, these elements are making use of the Internet. In addition to aforementioned sources as Thingiverse and Instructables, these are also great online sharing platforms:

- Make It @ Your library: Project database for making in libraries that contains content from Instructables, curated by a group of librarians: http://makeitatyourlibrary.org/.
- FabSchool contains curated maker projects from Instructables, but also how-to's from Youtube and Vimeo, with a special focus in maker education, and is a nice resource for libraries: http://fabschool.nl/.

DATA SOURCES

- FabLabs.io is the resource of the international FabLab community. It provides insight into the labs worldwide, as well as the machines they use: https://www.fablabs.io.
- The Maker Education Initiative's Resource Page: The website of the Maker Education Initiative is a great resource for anyone interested in making in education, but is also very useful for libraries: http://makered.org/resources/.
- Library Makers is a website maintained by a youth librarian of Madison Public Library that contains "somewhat non-traditional library programs I've created to take advantage of the one-on-one opportunities we have at the library today": http://librarymakers.blogspot.com/.
- Cybrary Man's makerspace resources page is maintained by retired educator Jerry Blumengarten and also features a lot of information about library makerspaces: http://cybraryman.com/makerspaces.html.
- Renovated Learning is a great resource for information about maker education, and is also very useful for library purposes. It is maintained by school librarian Diana Rendina: http://renovatedlearning.com/makerspace-resources/.

RECOMMENDED BOOKS AND MAGAZINES

- *Make:* magazine: iconic magazine featuring great maker projects: http://makezine.com/.
- *Invent to Learn: Making, Tinkering, and Engineering in the Classroom*: If you're thinking of providing maker workshops in your library, this book is essential. It covers everything from the history and pedagogy of making in the classroom to practical steps you can take to get started: http://www.inventtolearn.com/.
- *Makerspace Playbook*: Published by Maker Media and available as a free download, this book is very helpful in getting you started creating a makerspace: http://makerspace.com/wp-content/uploads/2013/02/MakerspacePlaybook-Feb2013.pdf.

- *The Makerspace Workbench: Tools, Technologies, and Techniques for Making*: Adam Kemp wrote this amazing resource (published by Maker Media) for everything related to setting up a maker space: http://www.makershed.com/products/the-makerspace-workbench.

All of these tools and resources are readily available online, most at no cost, and can become a vital part of your library collection. This largely open-source suite of tools creates an accessible way for both staff and patrons to become accomplished makers and for library makerspaces to become enjoyable and productive community resources.

NOTES

1. Fred "The Great Fredini" Kahl, "Full Body Scanning with the Scan-O-Tron 3000," *Make:*, http://makezine.com/projects/guide-to-3d-printing-2014/scan-o-tron-3000/ (accessed December 10, 2014).

2. "All about Laser Cutters: Overview," https://learn.adafruit.com/all-about-laser-cutters/overview (accessed December 10, 2014).

3. "Lasercutter—MiniFabLab," MiniFabLab, http://www.minifablab.nl/lasercutter/ (accessed December 10, 2014). Note: Bart Bakker, the owner of MiniFabLab and a longtime member of the international FabLab community, provided valuable information on the laser cutting part of this chapter. Bakker gives advice to Dutch and international FabLabs on what types of machines to purchase.

4

LIBRARY EXAMPLES AND CASE STUDIES

The largest online directory of library makerspaces currently shows there are now more than seventy throughout the country, providing evidence of robust growth in conceptual development of makerspaces in libraries.[1] The list includes academic libraries, small libraries with allocated spaces for 3D printers or art supplies, as well as massive spaces encompassing whole floors of libraries and featuring a wide variety of resources and functionality. Each space is designed to meet different interests or needs and accommodate patrons to the best of each library's ability. Many more libraries that don't have physical makerspaces are also exercising some unprecedented creative freedom in program development. All represent the cutting edge of twenty-first-century library evolution.

We'll take a look at a few of these innovative libraries here—some with full-blown makerspaces, others with nontraditional programming—and explore how they're organized and how they operate and consider some takeaways from each for your library.

LIBRARIES WITH MAKERSPACES

These libraries have carved some creative space out of their existing facilities or found a way to add functional "maker" space to their libraries. These types of library makerspaces typically feature the types of equipment and resources traditionally associated with private makerspaces: 3D printers, hand tools, some power tools, electronics equipment, specialized computers, sometimes CNC machines, and media equipment. We'll look at some well-recognized examples and some new and promising ones.

Fayetteville Free Library Fab Lab (New York State)

The Fayetteville Free Library (FFL) Fabulous Laboratory (Fab Lab; http://www.fflib.org/make/fab-lab) was developed to make technology more accessible to the general public. According to the FFL Fab Lab website, "There is no other place in New York that provides free and open access to 3D printing technology, which has the power to revolutionize society. The public library will provide a safe and accessible space where anyone in the community can interact, understand and develop through use of the technologies available in the space."

FFL makerspace programs are largely run by community volunteers who share the things they're passionate about and interested in with one another and their community. The balance of programs is run by library staff. Over time, the library moved away from paying outside experts to conduct programs as community members stepped up to share their own expertise and knowledge. The FFL Fab Lab offers three separate spaces: FFL Fab Lab Fabrication space, FFL Digital Creation Lab, and Little Makerspace for ages five to eight.

The Fabulous Lab offers a robust maker buffet, including multiple 3D printers and scanners, laser cutters, die-cut machines, several sewing machines and related textiles work tools and resources, general craft equipment, jewelry-making tools, hand tools, electronics equipment like soldering irons, multimeters, wire cutters and Arduino boards, PCs and Macs loaded with high-end development and multimedia software, and a variety of educational kits for loan. Kits are loaned out on a first-come-first-serve basis for twenty-one days with no renewals.

FFL executive director Sue Considine said the library took on the makerspace development as part of an effort "to shift our service from passive information consumption to content creation and fabrication, to help support knowledge exchange and new knowledge development in our community." FFL started at the most fundamental level in assessing their goals and their ability to meet them.

"We did a deep dive into our current operating budget, assessed the value of everything we were currently doing, and reallocated funds to do 'what's next.' We also actively sought community partners, in-kind services, and we won an award from a crowdsource funder," said Considine.

Community engagement is key to the FFL Fab Lab's success, acknowledges Considine.

> As quickly as possible, turn it over to the community. End goal: a community-defined and *community-led* space. Reach out into the community to identify the talent, skill sets, and enthusiasm that are already there, then provide the platform and access to resources to support neighbors teaching neighbors.

"Don't look for a kit!" says Considine. "Talk to your community, formally and informally, and listen. Their aspirations should drive your agenda."

Dorothy Lumley Melrose Center for Technology, Innovation and Creativity, Orlando Public Library, Florida

The Dorothy Lumley Melrose Center for Technology, Innovation and Creativity (http://tic.ocls.info/), in the Orlando Public Library, usually called the Melrose Center, is a 26,000-square-foot innovation center funded by a $1 million gift from the Kendrick B. Melrose Family Foundation in honor of Melrose's mother, Dorothy. In addition to the Melrose Family Foundation gift, the library contributed $1.5 million of its own funds to build and equip the center. The Melrose Center, which opened on February 8, 2014, occupies the second floor of the Orlando Public Library.

Recognized by the American Library Association as a "Library of the Future" before the Melrose Center opened, the new makerspace expands the role of the library, offering access to hardware, equipment, software, support, and programming "to inspire and invigorate creativity and accomplishment."

According to the Melrose Center mission statement, the role of the Melrose Center is not to compete with professional or formal education in the area, but to "serve the community by providing introductory and 'amateur' enthusiasts an opportunity for hands-on exploration, experimentation and experience. Whenever possible, we focus on the use of open source resources, so that our customers have the opportunity to replicate and practice."

The Melrose Center includes video and audio production studios, a photography studio, fabrication lab (FabLab), simulation lab, interactive media wall, conference room, and tech center. There are Macs and PCs available for use in the audio, photo, and video studios as well as in the public editing workstations. The Adobe Master Collection CS6, which will soon be upgraded to Adobe Creative Cloud, is available on computers. Autodesk educational and entertainment software packages are also available on the computers; the package includes Maya and AutoCAD.

In the simulation lab, there are full-size flight, driving, hydraulic excavator, and forklift simulators. For learning purposes, in the classroom, there are desktop simulators available for students to use. The FabLab has three 3D printers and a silhouette cutter. Other tools in the FabLab include soldering irons and electronic, engineering, and prototyping kits, such as Arduinos, littleBits, Snap Circuits, and K'NEX. The audio, photo, and video studios are fully equipped with professional-grade equipment. More information on specific equipment can be found at http://www.ocls.info/melrose under Services.

Orange County Library cardholders can use all the spaces free for one to three multi-hour sessions per week, depending on the space. Cost after the allotted free time is $25 per session. Out-of-district residents must take an orientation class to receive a Melrose card and can then use equipment and spaces at rates ranging from $25 to $100 per session.

Ormilla Vengersammy is the Technology and Education Center department head. She oversees the development and operations of the Melrose Center, as well as curriculum development for the Orange County Library System (OCLS) Technology Training Program. Currently, more than two hundred unique technology classes are taught in-person and online in three languages to patrons systemwide throughout the library district in Orange County, Florida.

Programming at the Melrose Center is driven by staff and the library's Adult Programs Department, as well as in partnership with community groups such as the Orlando Tech Association and local game development group Indienomicon. The Melrose Center has provided the impetus for a range of new programming.

"We have developed over seventy equipment and software classes," reported Vengersammy. "Twice a month we offer Tech Talk, our interactive presentation series. Community speakers come and share their knowledge, services, and experience with Melrose users."

Vengersammy feels that community involvement is critical to the Melrose Center's success. "In our experience, community and staff engagement is a must. While in the planning stages, we formed community and staff focus groups. The information gathered through these groups informed many of the decisions made in the development of the center. Engaging stakeholders from the very beginning has been incredibly benefiting to us."

The biggest challenge, she says, has been getting word out about the new public space. "Some people do not expect to find these services and resources at their library. Through strategic partnerships and by delivering great experiences to our users, word of the center has begun to spread. We have found that word of mouth is our best and most effective marketing tool."

The results are telling—and promising. Says Vengersammy:

> Upon the opening of the Center, there was a steady increase in door count for the first seven months. During our summer months, there was a rise in door count, and then a slight drop after school began. We have seen a steady number of users but do predict over the holidays there would be a drop, as we have seen systemwide over the years. We have been able to tie about seventy to ninety new library card registrations per month directly to the Center.

THE HIVE Community Innovation Center at the John F. Germany Public Library, Tampa, Florida

THE HIVE (http://www.hcplc.org/hcplc/locations/hve/), so called for a historic architectural feature that resembles a beehive, is a 10,000-square-foot public community innovation center and makerspace located on the third floor of the John F. Germany Public Library, the main branch of the Tampa-Hillsborough County Public Library System. The space got its start as a collaborative venture between the county and a local nonprofit in 2013.[2] Divergent goals ended the agreement and the

Code for Tampa Bay Brigade meeting at THE HIVE at John F. Germany Library in Tampa

library took full ownership of the space in the spring of 2014, bringing it back into alignment with the original mission and purpose of the space as a public creative makerspace. THE HIVE opened to the public officially in mid-November 2014.

"The goal of THE HIVE, as expressed through activities and services," said principal librarian Megan Danak, "is to emphasize creativity, collaboration, and coworking."

Danak, who is manager of THE HIVE and coordinator of the library system's public technology programs, said the library began looking at new ways to use space in 2012–2013 when the library system had several branches expanding or under construction.

> We were starting to look at adding more collaborative space, makerspaces, and "people space" to branches. Around that time, a nonprofit approached us to partner, create, and co-operate an innovation center at our main library in downtown Tampa. Although we parted ways with the nonprofit, the community was listening and excited about the new space. It's important to note that the idea for adding a

space like this initially came from interested community members. That's always the best starting point for any new library service— listening to and responding to your community.

The library listened and budgeted funds to build out the space and purchase equipment. Additional support from the Friends of the Library helps fund program and project supplies, additional equipment, and guest presenters.

THE HIVE consists of six separate but complementary areas: a makerspace with hand tools, workbenches, 3D printers, and desktop CNC machines; a media:scape collaborative work area; a robotics center with a permanent competition field suitable for K–12 *FIRST* Tech Challenge or VEX competition practice and training; a recording studio; flex meeting space; and an arts center with sewing machines, sergers, and a variety of arts and craft equipment.

Resources include an Inventables CNC milling machine, paper/vinyl cutter, Arduinos, littleBits, hand tools (screwdrivers, soldering irons, and wrenches that the public can use), sewing machines, sergers, and an embroidery machine, as well as a variety of sewing/needlework supplies and other craft supplies.

THE HIVE also features the library system's first Mac in the recording studio, with all of the native software, as well as ProTools and Adobe Creative Cloud. The studio includes a green-screen wall, studio lighting, a variety of microphones, a drum pad, a midi controller, and a video camera for public use. The facility also has projectors and screen casting capabilities.

THE HIVE offers bookable spaces and equipment, creative programming, and open learning labs for the public. Guests must have a valid Hillsborough County Public Library card to schedule use of bookable spaces and equipment, but programs and events are open to all. There is no cost to use the space or equipment.

The MakerBot 3D printers get a lot of use, said Danak. "We use a lot of open-source and web-based software for our 3D printing and modeling classes, like Tinkercad and Blender, and we've recently starting teaching 3D modeling classes for tablets, using free apps. The public response has been positive and enthusiastic."

We're thrilled with the excitement and energy the public has shown for the space. A community is growing—people are not only asking to use the spaces and resources, but they are offering their own expertise and knowledge to help others. They are not only attending our programs; they are key in planning and implementing programs as well. It's exciting to see people take ownership and want to contribute, as well as create, in the space.

The biggest challenge, according to Danak, was the immense scope of the effort:

> Kicking the door down with so much new technology and so many new services all at once was ambitious and continues to be a challenge. Fortunately we have excited and motivated staff eager to learn, lead the way, and try new things. We are still working on building awareness of the space and our services.

The library had to develop policies and procedures both for space use and equipment use, as well as entirely new user guidelines for the floor, due to the many spaces and the varied equipment offered.

> We could potentially have many different activities happening in THE HIVE at once, and we quickly realized that having one person at a traditional reference desk would not work in managing the space. So we had to work through a new way of scheduling staff, as well as space use. Safety is also a concern, and we worked with our county attorney and risk management department on liability waivers, since we invite the public to use tools that could be potentially dangerous. We also needed to develop safety guidelines, orientations and training, etc. As we are hoping to expand services developed in THE HIVE to other library branches, we tried to develop policies that we could apply systemwide—for example, for use of the 3D printers.

THE HIVE's ultimate goal is for the public to drive the programming, says Danak. The library is monitoring the use of services and space as they progress in order to gauge what the public is most interested in, whether it's 3D printing, filmmaking, sewing in the arts center, or some aspect of the makerspace.

"Currently our library-led events are intended to raise awareness, highlight and drive use of the resources and spaces available to the public, and we will continue to develop our programs based on public engagement and interests."

ACADEMIC LIBRARY MAKERSPACES

Seminole Community Library at St. Petersburg College, St. Petersburg, Florida

Seminole Community Library at St. Petersburg College, Seminole Campus (http://www.spcollege.edu/scl/), is a partnership between the college and the city of Seminole. It is a public library and a college library and home to the Innovation Lab, a public makerspace. The library is intended to be a "Community Commons" where connections are made between people and information. In addition to the Innovation Lab, the library has print, media, and electronic resources; the Connections Café; program rooms; an art gallery and rooms for classes, conferences, and reading; and functions as a cultural, academic, and networking hub in the greater Seminole area.

The library's Innovation Lab opened to the public in June 2014. Information services librarian Chad Mairn is also an assistant professor at St. Petersburg College and serves as Innovation Lab manager. He says his reasons for developing the Innovation Lab were somewhat selfish, which isn't a bad thing in the case of creative spaces; those who enjoy tinkering, and then create spaces for others to tinker with them, often draw in and inspire others to creative endeavors and broaden access for all, both of which have happened with the Innovation Lab.

"I like to play with technology and I figured it would be nice to create a space (i.e., a playground for people to color outside the lines) so that I can play with these new technologies more often. As a result, I submitted a grant to SPC's Foundation and got it!"

Additional funding to build out the space has come from a variety of different sources, including the college budget, private donations, and a library acquisitions budget. Lab resources currently include a Free-Fab3D Monolith 3D Printer built locally using other 3D printers; littleBits Synth Kit, Arduino Kit, Avid Fast Track Duo Audio Interface with Pro Tools Express; computers (an iMac, two Linux computers, and one Windows computer); a variety of open-source software applications for 3D printing, design, and so on; MaKey MaKey, Cubelets, ProtoSnap LilyPad, Raspberry Pi, Apollo Precision Tool Kit, Parallax Programmable Boe-Bot Robot Kit, Elenco Deluxe Learn to Solder Kit; Samsung 32-Inch 1080p LED HDTV with Logitech TV Cam HD for Skype Calls; Chromecast; Atari 1040ST computer running Notator music software; Kinect; and a reference collection including books and magazines.

The Innovation Center has leveraged those resources for some unique programming. "Our first workshop," said Mairn, "was to build a LibraryBox—an open-source online file distribution system that doesn't require Internet access. We are doing two Hour of Code events for Computer Science Education Week and have the Addy Award–winning Echo Bridge Pictures doing a lecture/workshop/art contest. The Innovation Lab has been asked to go outside the lab's walls and participate in the Suncoast Arts Fest to include a 'Maker Table' so the process of being creative using technology can be shown."

The biggest challenge Mairn has encountered is finding sufficient volunteer staffing to be open longer hours. But he's pleased with the response to the space by students and proud of the fact that the Innovation Lab "is a place for people to play and to feel comfortable making mistakes. People don't need to worry about grades in this lab and can think, learn, create, and share without feeling any pressure." Participation and creative use of the space has been steadily growing.

His most valuable piece of advice to those interested in creating similar spaces echoes that of other library makerspace managers: "Survey your users to see what they are really curious about and go with it. Include your users in decision making."

Grand Center Arts Academy Charter School Library Makerspace, St. Louis, Missouri

Grand Center Arts Academy (GCAA; https://gcaamakerspace. wordpress.com) is a St. Louis, Missouri, public charter middle and high school located in St. Louis's cultural arts district. The GCAA Makerspace was created in early 2013 as an "ideation lab"; the space takes up two-thirds of the school library and is available throughout the day for students to engage in open-ended creative exploration in engineering, design, and programming projects. The space is stocked with Arduinos, cardboard, simple circuitry, MaKey MaKey, Tinkercad, 3D printing, and vinyl cutting machines.

GCAA Makerspace manager Andrew Goodin isn't a librarian; he's the "Makerspace teacher." A chemist by degree, with a master's in education, Goodin is cofounder of the Disruption Department, an educational technology nonprofit that creates tangible STEAM learning opportunities for students from underresourced neighborhoods in St. Louis. He's been recognized as one of *St. Louis Business Journal*'s "30 Under 30" and awarded the St. Louis Science Center's Loeb Prize for Teaching Excellence, and he's passionate about GCAA Makerspace.

In addition to facilitating Makerspace orientation, maintaining and stocking tools and materials, and managing the Makerspace budget and grant program, he also develops instructional materials aligned with the Next Generation Science Standards and works to inspire and engage student creation and recruit community volunteers to help mentor students. The impetus behind developing the Makerspace in the library, said Goodin, was to better integrate their students' innate artistic skills with traditional coursework in their core classes.

"In initially piloting the Makerspace," Goodin said, "we were hoping to seamlessly add the 'arts' to STEAM, providing an approach to learning unparalleled in St. Louis."

They seem to have done just that.

Starting with a small-scale effort, targeting a small number of users with a budget of just $100, the program gradually scaled to access for the entire school through a variety of creative funding methods, from traditional school funding and grants, to a GoFundMe site, DonorsChoose, and various private and local sponsors. In 2014, GCAA received a $50,000 grant from the Disruption Department.

Originally, the GCAA Makerspace was only accessible to seventh graders one day a week. "On the first day," recalled Goodin, "students collaborated to determine the problems they'd like to address, materials that would be needed, and structure of the space. It was quickly determined that cardboard would be necessary for prototyping inventions. Thankfully, the GCAA custodians were willing to leave some in the room. It wasn't long before a huge stockpile had been acquired."

The $100 budget was used for various prototyping and storage materials, said Goodin, with which students prototyped a wide array of ideas focused on making school more "awesome." Given the success of the pilot program, the school committed to expand the Makerspace to a full-time program in the library for the 2013–2014 school year.

"In 2013–2014, the Makerspace took on a 'drop-in' model. Students from all grades were able to access the space before school, after school, and during their study hall. Four hundred unique students dropped in a total of ten thousand times throughout the course of the year designing projects of their choosing with a wide array of technology."

Now, due to popular demand for formal Makerspace programming from students, Goodin said, classes are held in the Makerspace, including a seventh-grade "Design Thinking 101" semester-long class, an eighth-grade "Make, Hack, Play" course, and a high school "STEAM Innovation Lab" course. All programming and curriculum is student driven.

In an article for EdSurge, Goodin observed, "The Makerspace creates a unique atmosphere for students to be active participants in creating their own knowledge. Because students are driven by the product they hope to create, they push themselves to learn whatever skills are necessary to make it a reality."[3]

Goodin's best practice recommendation is to start small. "We started with a budget of $100 and built momentum among key stakeholders. This resulted in a wave of support as we scaled up to a larger space."

The biggest challenge, he says, is adapting the space to the variety of student uses. "We have limited electrical outlets that are located in awkward places. We (students and me) are continually adapting the space to enhance productivity."

The results, Goodin says, have been well worth it. "The student response to our Makerspace has been incredible. A culture of collaboration and community has developed where students provide critical feedback and support to each other. When a student shows off a project, his or her peers are the first to provide excited praise. We've got a good energy." And they've got a school library space that's unique, precedent setting, and vigorously used.

INTERNATIONAL LIBRARY MAKERSPACES

YouLab, Pistoia, Italy

Formally known as YouLab Pistoia, An American Corner, YouLab (http://www.sangiorgio.comune.pistoia.it/youlab-pistoia-an-american-corner) is a collaborative project between the U.S. Embassy in Italy and the Library of San Giorgio di Pistoia to provide a public center for digital innovation. Pistoia, with a population of about ninety thousand residents, is a half hour from Florence and Pisa, located in the heart of Tuscany. The space is intended mainly for youth to have access to a rich set of audio-video equipment and computers to learn new skills, hone mastery across different environments and platforms, and be able to create digital products.

Maria Stella Rasetti, a head librarian at the Library of San Giorgio di Pistoia, where YouLab Pistoia is located, said the makerspace grew out of an effort by the U.S. Embassy in Rome in 2012 to find a partner to develop a digital makerspace.

"The goal was to create a new 'American Corner' in a public library based on the concept of a digital innovation center for youth," explained Rasetti.

> This digital innovation center fulfills the important goals stated in the U.S. State Department's Office of Global Youth Issues policy such as empowering young people as positive economic and political actors; encouraging governments to create enabling environments for youth; engaging young people in U.S. Embassy public diplomacy programs.
>
> Our library was chosen by the U.S. Embassy as the best partner for the project because it was considered highly integrated in the local community, characterized by a strong commitment to free public access, and could be able to share the vision that young people need education and guidance to successfully navigate the new digital economy.

The U.S. State Department earmarked $50,000 U.S. in 2013 for the project and another $25,500 U.S. to buy equipment. The library came up with its own funding for furniture, promotion, and maintenance; all the staff, including the makerspace coordinator, librarians, and civil servants working as makerspace mentors, are teachers. The makerspace is run as a special project of the public library by the library director, with all the events and activities held at YouLab included as part of library programs.

The space includes sixteen tablets (Android, Windows, Apple) and two drawing tablets, digital photo and video cameras (professional and consumer level) and movie set equipment (video accessories, lighting kit, etc.), Arduino, 3D printer, two LEGO Mindstorms kits, Silhouette Cameo cutting machine, cutter plotter (professional level), ten PCs in the computer lab, and a variety of creative software: Adobe Suite, Auto-CAD, Windows, as well as several open software systems. The library is also stocking books both in Italian and in English about the topics of YouLab. Youth are the main focus of the makerspace, said Rasetti, but programming is provided for all ages.

> We have developed a lot of programs on a daily basis: courses and classes on videomaking, photography making, web programming (each course about twenty-four hours, twice a week for six weeks); how-to classes on Prezi, Facebook, Twitter, LinkedIn, Scratch, Google Suite, Creative Commons Licenses, Open Office Software, Arduino kits, 3D printing. The most popular courses are devoted to people who want to improve their skills on how to use tablets, apps, and mobile devices in general. We created also an Emergency Room Program for Computer Skills, quite popular among seniors.

The library also provides classes for youth on 3D creative digital objects, regularly filling a monthly course on how to create earrings with the 3D printer, offered as part of a STEM program for girls.

"A special edition of this program was connected to a European Project on creative promotion of Cultural Heritage: a group of ten- to thirteen-year-old kids created a new app, BiblioPT (downloadable for free from Android market and from Apple Store), with the story of the libraries in our town. During the story they show some 3D models of curious 'library objects' discovered in the libraries."

3D printers are also popular with single young adults. "The most popular instrument is the 3D printer," stated Rasetti, "used for free by students for their graduation final work in architecture and art. Single users have been interested in using our 3D printers for re-creation of broken home tools."

Rasetti has a few best practices recommendations:

- Create a dedicated team inside the library to manage events and makerspace opportunities.
- Look for alliances with teachers, experts, nerds, and other "human resources" in your community and in your library for sharing skills.
- Create a makerspace that "belongs to everyone" instead of simply being considered a new section of the library.
- The library coordinator must be able to share the "power" of managing makerspace programs.
- Create logical bridges between digital and physical making. "It's wonderful to create a flower with the drawing tablet in the maker-space, and then to embroider it on a handkerchief."
- Be curious and remember the fifth Ranganathan Law[4]: The library is a growing organism.

Rasetti advises against considering the makerspace as "a separate section" of the library, but rather to let it "invade" the library with its activities, opportunities, and "state of mind."

"Don't think that your energies spent in the makerspace activities impoverish the traditional library activities," she says. "Let the maker-space 'nourish' the library."

At YouLab, the library is nourished in some very meaningful ways. At the end of their longer programs, they create small teams within which each member of the team "returns" the energy of what he or she learned, "creating in a collaborative way a new digital object which becomes part of the YouLab heritage and identity." YouLab's website was created as the final exercise by the attendees of a high-level course on web programming, providing a powerful way for those served by the makerspace to serve the makerspace, building community and pride of ownership.

FryskLab, Bibliotheekservice Fryslân, Leeuwarden, The Netherlands

FryskLab (http://www.frysklab.nl/) is an initiative of Bibliotheekservice Fryslân (Library Service Friesland, or BSF).[5] Fryslân is a province in the northwest of the Netherlands, and FryskLab, housed in a former library bus, is Europe's first mobile library FabLab. The goal of Frysk-

FryskLab, the Netherlands

Lab is to explore how a mobile FabLab contributes to the creative, technical, and entrepreneurial skills development of children and young people.

Aan Kootstra works at Bibliotheekservice Fryslân as a digital domain specialist and is the lab manager of FryskLab. After studying some examples from the United States, Kootstra said BSF was excited to strengthen the relationship between FabLab and the libraries of Fryslân.

"With our mobile lab," he explained, "we want to contribute to the innovative capacity of the province. Technology will play an increasingly important role in our society. With the democratization of technology machines are becoming more affordable and in affordable range of citizens. Libraries can play a major role in familiarizing citizens with this technology."

"The availability of digital fabrication," Kootstra said, "is changing the role of individuals from consumer to producer, and libraries are well positioned to develop the types of programs that can stimulate that evolution." FryskLab focuses on educational programming developed around local issues like water technology and sustainability, which they combine with digital fabrication technology. Due to the rural nature of Fryslân, a mobile lab was employed to provide greater outreach and access.

FryskLab is funded mostly through project grants, with the Leeuwarden municipality financing the bus and the province of Friesland contributing for the purchase of machines and other equipment. The educational package was developed by a contribution from the private fund Fonds21, the Pica Foundation funds their linked open data project, and the series *Fab the Library!* is made possible by a contribution from The Netherlands Institute for Public Libraries (SIOB). The mobile FabLab is equipped with three 3D printers and a 3D scanner, laser cutter, vinyl cutter, hand tools, 3Doodler pen, ten Macbook Airs, Apple TV, MaKey MaKeys, Arduinos and littleBits kits, Strawbees, and a variety of software including Scratch, Doodle3D, Cura, Repetier, 123Design, Inkscape, Photoshop Elements, Tinkercad, SketchUp Make, Sculptris, and Mozilla Webmaker.

FryskLab has developed a number of programs related to the mobile FabLab. FryskLab Elements, a program for children and teens (ages ten to eighteen), teaches digital fabrication in relation to water technology, sustainable energy, and new craftsmanship. *Fab the Library!* (see chapter 2) instructs librarians about makerspaces, and Medialiteracy-Makers! is a media- and web-literacy program in which teachers and librarians will create their own media literacy offerings within Mozilla Webmaker.

FryskLab's Open Product Design Challenges provide some real-world skills development from prototype to pitch, says Kootstra.

"Students work on a real business problem. Design thinking methods such as the Business Model Canvas or Empathy Mapping are used by the students to find a solution to the problem. This will result in a prototype which will be fabricated in the lab and used in the product pitch for the client and classmates. In this program, all facets of digital manufacturing and twenty-first-century skills will come into fruition."

Kootstra advises collaborating wherever possible, in the development of makerspaces and related programming: "Often there are Fab-Labs, hackerspaces, or makerspaces around who know which programs and machines are suitable for a library FabLab. Also try to find early support across your own organization."

Skaparbibblan, Vaggeryd, Sweden

Vaggeryd is a small town in Sweden of about five thousand residents. The Vaggeryd Library is an integrated high school and public library; and library manager Lo Claesson, inspired by the library-based maker movement in the United States, saw immediate collaborative possibilities between area schools, libraries, and businesses and how well Vaggeryd's vision compared with the makerspace concept.[6]

"I listened to David Lankes in 2011," Claesson recalled and "read about makerspaces in the U.S. and thought makerspaces were a good way to fulfill the mission of the library and librarians according to Lankes."

The new creative space in the library was funded regionally and through the support of local businesses. The space features MakerBots, different kinds of sewing machines, Arduino, LEGO Mindstorms, 4D Frame, littleBits and MaKey MaKey kits, conductive thread and LED lamps (sew electric), and software like Scratch, Kojo, Solid Works, and some free CAD software, and Creative Suite, along with woodworking equipment.

The space is mostly used by groups so far, says Claesson, "but we have 3D cafés and 'the pupil's choice,'" where students can choose from different activities a couple of hours each week. The makerspace also hosts a Geek Girls Club for girls ages ten to thirteen and programming Kojo for kids.

Claesson counsels moderation in the development of a library makerspace. "Don't buy too many things immediately. Let the maker space emerge gradually. Do not compete with other businesses, but try to co-operate."

NONTRADITIONAL PARTNERSHIPS

MakersBuzz, Tilburg, the Netherlands

MakersBuzz is another mobile FabLab that tours around libraries and schools in Tilburg in The Netherlands. It's the product of a collaborative agreement between the province of Noord-Brabant and Cubiss, a consultancy office for the libraries in the provinces of Noord-Brabant and Limburg.

Neeltje van Helvoort, a consultant ICT at Cubiss, coordinates the MakersBuzz with a team of five other colleagues, visiting libraries and schools with the MakersBuzz.

"With the MakersBuzz," he said, "we give libraries the opportunity to experience the power and attraction of digital fabrication to their citizens."

MakersBuzz is funded for its first three years through the provincial assignment by the library. From 2015 on the MakersBuzz will also be used in the province Limburg as part of the provincial educational assignment to libraries and Cubiss. MakersBuzz contains 3D printers (three), a laser cutter, a vinyl cutter, MaKey MaKey and a BeeBot, and an assortment of tools.

"Usually we take one 3D printer, MaKey MaKey, and the BeeBot into the building of the library or the school," explained van Helvoort. "This makes it possible to reach more people and a broader audience, both in the MakersBuzz and in the library or school."

MakersBuzz is used by citizens of all ages, with a focus on short activities to learn about the equipment and about the ways to design and fabricate. In 2015, van Helvoort said, MakersBuzz will include special programs for the highest classes of primary school and for preparatory secondary vocational education.

Educators are already taking notice. "A school board of eighteen schools for primary education in a big city in Noord-Brabant invited the MakersBuzz to a seminar for its five hundred teachers," recalled van Helvoort. "The staff of the MakersBuzz gave several workshops to the teachers in which they learned about the equipment and the possibilities of the equipment in relation to the curriculum. They were very enthusiastic and saw a lot of ways to integrate the MakersBuzz in their curriculum."

Van Helvoort recommends collaboration wherever possible. "Don't try to do this all alone," he says. "Make the connection with other people and organizations that are busy with makerspaces or who want to collaborate. Initiate one. Learn from each other. Benefit from the experience of others. Share your own experiences."

Valby FabLab, Copenhagen, Denmark

The Copenhagen FabLab opened in January 2013 on the fourth floor of the Valby Cultural Center at Toftegårds Square, in the southwestern corner of Copenhagen, as a "free, open and creative playground with an exciting machine park for anyone with good ideas."[7]

Copenhagen FabLab was created to give citizens free access to modern 2D and 3D technologies that make it quick and easy to turn their ideas into concrete realities. The space is open seven days a week and accessible by all citizens through their Public Health Security Card and a PIN code, which they get at their local library.

Rasmus Fangel Vestergaard is the library liaison at the Copenhagen FabLab, which operates as a collaborative effort of the library, local public schools, and Valby Culture. The space was funded by local supporters. Copenhagen FabLab at Valby currently runs two programs, says Vestergaard: FabSchool, initially aimed at a local school but now rolled out to a greater part of area public schools, and FabCreation, a two-week-long free program designed for people looking for work or educational opportunities.

"We're also one of the most open official FabLabs in the world," reports Vestergaard, "as we have combined the openness of libraries with the facilities and ideology of the FabLab. It's self-serviced access between 8 a.m. and 22 p.m. every day. Just use your library card."

The Copenhagen FabLab houses a CNC machine, 3D printers, a laser cutter, video facilities, 3D scanner, plotter, digital embroidery machine, sewing machines, electronic station, soldering station, and Arduinos.

For others looking at developing a library FabLab, Vestergaard advises, "Leave it open and think long term."

Too many maker projects run out of funding after two years, he says, because developers fail to take the long view.

> Providing access and re-accustoming people to their production means is an ever ongoing task for libraries. It just so happens that we've moved from physical to digital to tangible knowledge in the way and form we can mediate. . . .
>
> Is it my task as a librarian to teach others how to build a bed? I'd rather take the responsibility on how to guide others how to find the

information about how to build that bed, even though if it comes in the form of an .stl file.

Vestergaard loves that empowered peer-to-peer quality of the Fab-Lab in Valby, recalling how space users fixed some machinery after he left a note that it was broken.

"Pure magic!" he says.

The Waiting Room, Colchester, United Kingdom

The Waiting Room (http://commonlibraries.cc/the_waiting_room/) is a "library-hack-makerspace," collaboratively managed by the Creative Co-op and Colchester School of Art in conjunction with a wider group of stakeholders and creative professionals who live and work in or near St. Botolph's, in Essex, England, and in agreement with the Essex County Council's public library service.

Annemarie Naylor is the director of common futures at the Waiting Room, providing stakeholder management for the Waiting Room with its national partners.

The impetus for starting the Waiting Room, said Naylor, was "to prototype the library of the future in community hands, respond to calls from the creative community in Colchester for an appropriate space, and demonstrate the potential for integrated library-hack-makerspaces to add value to more straightforward co-location propositions."

The Waiting Room is intended to be a prototype of the "Common Library," a patron-driven effort "to empower people to co-design and deliver new library services in our increasingly open-source society, such that they are responsive to technological advancements and fast-changing local needs."[8] The Waiting Room is a "test-bed for library service transformation."[9]

Initial funding for the Waiting Room came from the Arts Council England, the Government's Portas Pilot program, the European Union's CURE Programme, Colchester Borough Council, Locality, and the Carnegie UK Trust. Today, the Waiting Room generates earned income from a bar, kitchen, café, community workshop membership fees, some retail, and resident studio rentals that are helping the space become self-sustaining. The Waiting Room features a workshop with standard tools, a letterpress and type/print room, a dark room for photography, facilities for silk-screen printing, a vinyl cutter, and Wi-Fi.

There is a wide range of users who, between September 2013 and February 2014, numbered more than six thousand. "In addition to regular creative users who avail themselves of the facilities during evenings and at weekends," said Naylor, "older people are supported by Age UK and other local stakeholders to use the space during the day time, we host a dedicated youth night, and regular Maker Wednesdays attract a broad spectrum of users from the community."

Naylor states that the key to success is listening to library stakeholders. "Build upon the fine grain of your community. Do not design/establish a makerspace 'top down.' Ensure you coproduce the space with users and help obtain and manage the tools they want, understand how to use and can teach others to use, and can also maintain in-house at low cost."

The main way public libraries could borrow approaches from the Waiting Room is in using space for activities that combine the sharing of knowledge, learning of new skills, and supporting enterprise in highly communal and sociable ways, says Naylor.

> This goes from social learning and knowledge sharing, to practical crafts and skills, to activities around arts, local history, culture and food. Moreover, since this project's inception in 2013, we have seen a growing interest in bringing 'making,' 'maker' events, and FabLabs into libraries to support enterprise, STEM skills, economic resilience, and build community connections. In this respect, there may be benefit in public libraries replicating Waiting Room inspired events rather than starting from scratch.

CREATIVE PROGRAMMING

If you don't have physical or personnel bandwidth, or perhaps administrative buy-in, for an actual makerspace, "pop-up" maker programming can help meet creative needs and interests in an affordable and interesting way. (See chapter 5, for more "pop-up" makerspace resources.)

Making without Makerspace: Folkelab, Aarhus Public Library, Denmark

Folkelab (http://folkelab.dk/english), or the People's Lab, is a two-year project of the Aarhus Public Library in Denmark. The project's aim is to explore how libraries, in collaboration with various partners, can create open innovation environments. Inspired by makerspaces and hackerspaces, the People's Lab seeks to "transfer and translate thoughts and experiences from Maker Spaces to a library context."

"We started out as a development project investigating how making, maker culture, and libraries could fit together," explained Louise Overgaard, project team leader. "We created six prototypes, like Techlab, Wastelab, and Mini Makerfaire. From the project we concluded that libraries can work with making without having a physical makerspace and now that is how we work."

Folkelab makes things, Overgaard pointed out, but they don't have a makerspace. A FabLab might be in their future, "but now we do making without makerspace."

> It makes sense to us because making is an approach to learning, sharing, and building collaborative relations more than the machines and the space. In our adult section we run making activities as a part of the regular services and have a 3D printer in the middle of the adult library. In the children's library we do pop-up makerspaces with creative activities and the initiative Coding Pirates once a week.

Program funding comes partly from the library budget, but mostly they educate staff to support maker activities and have a healthy complement of volunteers. Equipment is modest, consisting of a 3D printer, MaKey MaKey and littleBits kits, Arduino, LEGO Mindstorms, and hand-craft supplies, for things like their "hack-a-book" sessions. Public participation varies depending on the activity offered, said Overgaard.

"We have things for children, for children and families, for more hand-craft-interested adults and for more techie adults. . . . We use the library as a gate to making and new technologies—letting people be surprised over a 3Dprinter, etc."

Overgaard's signature piece of advice? "You need to focus more on people than machines. You need to focus on the ideas and the motivation and go from there on to teach people the skills." And be sure to involve your staff.

Maker Space in a Box: Maker Boxes, Åke Nygren, Stockholm Public Library, Sweden

Åke Nygren works at Stockholm Public Library at the Digital Library Department. He describes himself as a digital freelancer, library maker and activist, presenter, lifelong learner and explorer, and Mozillarian. Nygren is the originator of Maker Boxes (http://www.mozillarian.org), an independent and mobile concept.

"The reason I started," said Nygren, "was that I wanted to gather all sorts of portable material for making and tinkering to try out for myself and colleagues, friends, and others in the library business to experiment with. A long-term goal is to launch the Maker Boxes as a mobile event concept for the public."

Since the concept didn't fit entirely within the current mission of his library department, Nygren continues developing Maker Boxes as a freelancer, outside of his day job at Stockholm Public Library. He does this by giving paid presentations and workshops that could cover the costs for buying the material inside the boxes: Arduino, Raspberry Pi, E-textile material (including Adafruit), MaKey MaKey, littleBits, Strawbees, homemade conductive play dough, Bristlebot components, a drone, Library Box, knitting yarn, and the tools of Mozilla Webmaker: X-Ray Googles, Thimble, Mozilla Appmaker, and Popcorn Maker.

Participants in Maker Box workshops so far are librarians, library managers, high school teachers, and managers. Soon he will try out the concept with the public, as a library maker party.

"Start small!" is Nygren's main advice for libraries that want to start with making. "Invite users to become advisors and mentors; look for strategic partnership outside of the library business, such as academia, entrepreneurs, schools and passionate individuals. Also use all kinds of material, both from 'masculine' environments such as electronics and from 'female' contexts like textile."

Nygren also urges patience. "Building a maker space is making a community and networking and community building takes time! Don't talk too much about products, but rather themes and functionality: so coding, not Scratch, and social media, not Facebook."

Nygren's best-practice example is from a maker workshop with library managers in Alvesta, Sweden. Here he started tinkering first and explained the theory afterward: "The surprise effect of the Maker Boxes used boosted the curiosity among the participants. The content was secret and they had to investigate the material by themselves, solve the 'mystery,' without knowing the name of the product. I also used a bit of gamification to make people engaged and prevent a passive approach toward the challenges of the workshop."

FIRST Teams in Libraries

There's a significant and successful precedent for *FIRST* team development in libraries that has garnered both fiscal and community support across the nation.[10] The Haslet Public Library Robotics Club, in Chicago, won a $5,000 Loleta D. Fyan grant from the American Library Association in March 2014.[11] Also in the spring of 2014, Science Technology Activities and Resources Library Education Network (STAR Net) piloted a Jr. *FIRST* LEGO League (Jr. FLL) program with two libraries in Colorado and one in Wyoming.[12]

The initial program created fifteen teams that served eighty-three youth ages six through nine. Each of the three libraries recruited and trained coaches, registered teams, and held an eight-week team meeting season and an expo at the end. One library in the program broke its overall attendance record for a library-hosted community event with their Jr. FLL Expo. The second phase of the project will engage seventeen additional libraries for a total of eighty-five new teams in 2014–2015.

We'll look at a couple of library *FIRST* robotics programs in a little more depth here.

FRC Team Edgar Allan Ohms, Land O' Lakes Branch Library, Florida

Paul Stonebridge, teen services manager for the Pasco County Library System in Florida, along with library administrator Sean McGarvey, fielded a *FIRST* Robotics Competition (FRC) team at the Land O' Lakes (LOL) Public Library. The Edgar Allan Ohms team made headlines in March 2014 when they built a 120-pound robot at the library and went on to compete at the Orlando FRC Regional, placing solidly in the middle of a field of sixty-four teams.[13] They received funding support from the Pasco Economic Development Council for their second year.

"We started *FIRST* teams at the library to allow youth to learn more about robotics. *FIRST* teams give young people a chance to explore the world of science, tech, and engineering in a fun and friendly environment. The program also promotes digital literacy skills, critical thinking, and project-based learning," explained McGarvey.

Stonebridge said they felt the *FIRST* team would help with their mission to provide technology education and engagement for the public. And they were excited about creating the first library-based FRC team.

FIRST Robotics Competition can be an expensive program, with a first-year budget of $10,000 to $15,000. *FIRST* typically facilitates rookie team grants and makes other grants available as well. The LOL Library team applied for everything that was available and received a NASA grant, along with assistance from local businesses and from *FIRST* staff, who helped locate support. They also made technology improvements at the library to save money and asked the county for permission to use budget funds on the team, which they received.

Having a robotics team in the library necessitated some nontraditional programming, including working with mentors and staff to introduce student team members to CAD software and computers, Photoshop, Zbrush, 3D printing, and the use of basic power tools, in addition to low-level arts and crafts related to team spirit and marketing needs.

The library developed some interesting best practices for keeping students engaged, said McGarvey. "We offer a gift certificate drawing for all participant students who maintain a GPA above 3.2 for every semester they are involved with the team to encourage focus."

The library-based robotics program has captured the interest and imagination of the community and the library staff, who cheer on the robotics team and promote it to the public. Many staff members, they say, participate in robot-related functions.

For other libraries interested in developing *FIRST* robotics programming, McGarvey says, "Secure your workspaces and public support as far in advance as possible and have incentive packages ready to offer sponsors on the spot."

Aside from the high school team members, say Stonebridge and McGarvey, students of all ages have enjoyed the robot via demonstration programs for special library and school events, and the library is now teaching a "coder dojo" class for preteens to learn the basics of coding, as well as starting an informal LEGO robotics program in the library system for elementary and middle school students. The library is also in the process of carving out an actual makerspace, providing more workspace for the robotics team as well as for the general public.

The New Braunfels Public Library in San Antonio, Texas

New Braunfels takes the "everything is bigger in Texas" concept to heart with their *FIRST* program, hosting five Jr. *FIRST* LEGO League teams, six *FIRST* LEGO League teams, and one *FIRST* Tech Challenge (FTC) high school team, providing robotics programming for more than one hundred students a week. The FTC team actually competed in Australia one year.[14]

Kit Ward-Crixell, now youth services librarian at Port Townsend Public Library, said she started the *FIRST* robotics program at New Braunfels because she was looking for programs to appeal to upper-elementary and middle school students. The Friends of the Library provided initial support and the team received additional support from local engineering businesses.

While they have strong community support and a robust program, not everyone at New Braunfels is sold on the idea of robots in the library.

"A small minority of the group that provides our funding is not convinced of the value of our *FIRST* programs," says Megan Clark, the current youth services library technician and robotics coordinator at New Braunfels Public Library. "We are doing what we can to illustrate the importance of continuing the program, including asking current team members to speak to the group about their experiences and what they have gained."

The library is now in its fourth season of hosting *FIRST* teams, and their twelve teams serve more than one hundred youth, ages six to eighteen, with a comprehensive suite of tools and resources including more than fifteen laptops, LEGO EV3 and NXT Mindstorms kits and programming software, LEGO Tetrix parts, LabVIEW software, standard LEGO bricks, word processing and presentation software, graphic design software, Google Drive services, an Afina 3D printer with SketchUp, WordPress, and a range of power tools.

"We run our programs concurrently with the competition season, generally from August to March. In the off season, we provide additional programming and instruction on building robots and writing computer programs," notes Clark.

She feels they've successfully streamlined the process of getting teams up and running. They run mandatory summer workshops for team members to teach basic skills and host coach orientation and training meetings, especially helpful for rookie coaches.

"As the team coordinator, I provide weekly agendas a few days before teams meet for practice to help keep everyone on the same track. I also manage as much of the administrative side as possible to take the pressure off the parent volunteers who are coaching the teams directly. It definitely pays to delegate and divide the work!"

As far as best practices go, Ward-Crixell says, "When hosting *FIRST* teams: recruit, recruit, recruit!"

Recruit from the community for student team members, as well as for volunteer coaches and mentors. And make sure everyone is clear on expectations and requirements.

"To participate in our competitive robotics teams, members have to commit to a certain level of attendance and participation. Ensure all participants understand the requirements of the program, especially the researching and public speaking components. Familiarize yourself with the programming software and the LEGO technic construction sets."

Maximize collaboration, add the librarians. "Don't be afraid to reach out to other teams, near or far. *FIRST* is a very inclusive, welcoming program, and teams are generally happy to share advice, equipment, etc."

Remember, too, that it's not about winning, but about learning and discovery. "As long as the kids have fun, you've done well!"

NOTES

1. "Library Makerspaces—A Map of Library Makerspaces," Make It @ Your Library, http://www.makeitatyourlibrary.org (accessed November 4, 2014).

2. THE HIVE makerspace was designed by coauthor Terri Willingham and her husband, Steven.

3. Andrew Goodin, "Building Student Agency in a St. Louis Makerspace," EdSurge, October 9, 2014, https://www.edsurge.com/n/2014-10-09-building-student-agency-in-a-st-louis-makerspace (accessed December 3, 2014).

4. S. R. Ranganathan, *The Five Laws of Library Science*, 2nd ed. Bombay: Asia Pub. House, 1963.

5. *Makerspaces in Libraries* coauthor Jeroen de Boer is the project leader for the FryskLab Project.

6. Helen Andersson, "Skaparbibblan I Vaggeryd (Creates Bibblan Vaggeryd)," Skaparbibblan I Vaggeryd, April 2, 2014, http://www.framsidan.net/2014/04/skaparbibblan-i-vaggeryd/ (accessed December 18, 2014).

7. "Copenhagen Citizens Have Free Access to Ideudfoldelse in New Fab-Lab," Ingeniøren, January 8, 2013, http://ing.dk/blog/koebenhavns-borgere-faar-fri-adgang-til-ideudfoldelse-i-nyt-fablab-135382 (accessed December 18, 2014).

8. Common Libraries, http://commonlibraries.cc/about/ (accessed December 18, 2014).

9. Carnegie UK Trust, "Enterprising Libraries: The Waiting Room Case Study," 2014, http://www.carnegieuktrust.org.uk/publications/2014/enterprising-libraries-the-waiting-room-case-study (accessed December 9, 2014).

10. Katie Boyer, "Robotics Clubs at the Library," Public Libraries Online, http://publiclibrariesonline.org/2014/06/robotics-clubs-at-the-library/ (accessed June 25, 2014).

11. Norman Rose, "Haslet Public Library's Robotics Club Wins 2014 Loleta D. Fyan Grant," American Library Association, http://www.ala.org/news/press-releases/2014/03/haslet-public-library-robotics-club-wins-2014-loleta-d-fyan-grant (accessed June 25, 2014).

12. N. Peter, "STAR Library Education Network (STAR_Net) and Junior FIRST LEGO (Jr. FLL) Grant Opportunity—Deadline April 4, 2014," It's Time . . . NJ State Library, http://marketing.njstatelib.org/events/2014_04_04_040000/star_library_education_network_star_net_and_junior (accessed June 25, 2014).

13. Daylina Miller, "Robotics Team Builds One for the Books," *Tampa Tribune*, April 30, 2014.

14. Drew Stone, "Robotics Team in International Contest," *New Braunfels Herald Zeitung*, June 29, 2013.

5

STEP-BY-STEP LIBRARY PROJECTS

The best part of having a library makerspace is that you get to make stuff! Before librarians can embrace maker culture, though, they have to understand it. The best way to do that is for library staff and volunteers to get some firsthand experience with the types of programming and projects for which makerspaces are known.

For libraries, giving staff the opportunity to explore creative programming and to discover and build upon their own innate skills and interests can directly translate into empowered and impassioned librarians who can reinvigorate library programming and have a great time doing it. The following projects are presented in the style of Instructables or Make It @ Your Library (you'll learn about both here) and are designed to provide a wide range of activities and creative programming for library staff and patrons that can enrich the lives of both and enhance library experiences for everyone involved.

HOST A MAKE IT @ YOUR LIBRARY DAY

Planning for a "Make It @ Your Library Day" is a great way to introduce library staff and volunteers to maker culture and inspire more ideas for creative programming for patrons. Make It @Your Library is a popular website produced in collaboration with Instructables[1] and the American Library Association. The site began as a part of Illinois Libraries Explore, Apply and Discover (ILEAD) USA, an Institute of

Museum and Library Sciences (IMLS) grant-funded library program created "with the intention of helping librarians realize makerspace projects in their communities."[2]

Today, Make It @ Your Library is a popular and useful website with hundreds of projects, an informative blog, a library of resources, and a growing library makerspace directory. And it's also a great tool for a creative, hands-on, user-friendly introduction to maker culture. Before you embark, though, it's a good idea to get everyone thinking about what it is to "make" and to discover what library staff naturally enjoy creating.

Step 1: Take Stock of Staff Interests

Take some time to find out what staff members really like to do when they're not working and not reading. Some may be avid gamers—board, card, or video games. Others may have craft hobbies like quilting or painting. Some might belong to special interest clubs or organizations. Some may be movie buffs.

Having this conversation about what library staff does when not at work sets a more dynamic stage for exploring the concept of "making," conceptually moving discussion from requirements-driven work to interest-driven living. The idea is to experience the opportunity to ask—and be asked—not just, "What do you like to read?" but also "What do you like to do?"

Step 2: Take Stock of Community Culture

What staff likes to do may be, in large measure, influenced by community culture and trends. Rural library communities may be more agricultural in nature. Suburban library communities may have an active sports culture. Urban communities may be more focused on the arts or music or be more entrepreneurial in nature. Libraries in poor, underserved areas will obviously have a different cultural dynamic than libraries in affluent neighborhoods. Local hobbies and recreational activities will reflect neighborhood dynamics. Integrating community interests with staff interests will add another level of instructive experience to the hands-on projects.

Step 3: Pick a Project!

The Make It @ Your Library site provides a nice way to select appropriate projects for particular library environments and user skill sets. Projects are color coded,[3] ranging from "activity ready" simple, short projects to "dirty tool ready" projects that are complex, employ big tools, and generate noise. Projects can also be selected by age appropriateness, theme, cost, and amount of time required for completion.

Things to take into consideration when selecting or planning a project include:

- Work Space Configuration: If you already run craft programs at your library, you probably already have working spaces and protocols. "Maker" projects, however, often range outside the scope of traditional arts and crafts and may also require access to hand tools, electrical power, ventilation, a shop vac, and other supplies that may not be commonly used. Consider your resources when selecting a project and plan accordingly.
- Materials Costs: Paper and textiles projects may have modest costs; electronic projects or woodworking projects will have considerably higher expenses that have to be taken into consideration. Will the project require batteries? LEDs? Do you have enough 3D printer filaments? Don't just look at the finished product; review the full list of materials and budget out in advance.
- Preparation Time: Some projects require little more than paper and scissors. Others may require advance preparation, like cooking up dough, creating related materials or supply kits for participants, or stocking glue or soldering wire. Organizers should themselves run through a project first before rolling it out to participants so there are no surprises.
- Project Complexity: A companion consideration to preparation time is project complexity. While a finished project might look terrific online, pay attention to the "Time per Project" category and add an hour more for your first effort. You don't want to pick a project that's too easy. But you also don't want participants to become frustrated because of insufficient preparation or because a project is so far outside the scope of anyone's interest or ability.

work-arounds on budget limitations. Home improvement stores often provide gift cards or deep discounts to nonprofits and community groups, allowing cost-effective acquisition of supplies. Arts and crafts and electronic supply stores can provide similar nonprofit support. It may also be possible to partner with local suppliers and hardware stores, which will provide free or discounted supplies in exchange for recognition or as a community service.

Step 5: Pick Your Project

Select a project appropriate to available space, resources, budget, and staff. It's important that the selected project be achievable but not so simple as to seem patronizing to participants. Consider a project that brings added value to the library: things like a special table, display rack, shelving, artwork, signage, charging stations, lighting, tool holders, workbenches, outdoor displays, garden items, seating, or anything that can be considered a point of pride for makers and for the library.

Ultimately, the idea here is to provide another way for people to look at libraries and to inspire people to active creation, and if the creation actually serves some useful purpose, so much the better. Using pop-up makerspace projects to beautify or enhance the library serves not only to better engage the public, but also to improve chances of Friends' and local government support of potential future makerspace-related changes.

Step 6: Invite Patron Participation

After deciding on the project, put together a Call for Makers inviting public participation. Decide ahead of time on recommended ages for a project and how many people the library can comfortably accommodate. If there's a good chance there's going to be a lot of interest, consider multiple build teams and do two or more of the same project. Be clear on expectations and skill sets, identifying the types of tools that will be used during the build and whether the project will require basic, intermediate, or experienced tool use; how to dress (closed-toed shoes, etc.); and how much time the project is intended to take.

Step 7: Plan Your Work, and Work Your Plan

It's often a good idea for the project staff to do the build themselves first before inviting public participation. That way there's a more realistic sense of the actual time involved, as well as complexities that may not be evident in the build instructions. This also helps staff better guide the public build and have the correct supplies on hand, as well as a sample end product.

Instructables can be customized to suit the preferences or needs of a library, so feel free to remove steps that seem unnecessary or add some in where it might be helpful. Make sure all the necessary materials are available the day of the build, from safety glasses and fasteners and other consumables to first-aid supplies. If it's more than a one-day build, make sure everything is stored in such a way that the project can be picked up right where it left off previously.

Step 8: Document and Share

Take photos along the way and videotape. If the project is part of an Instructables contest, documentation will be required. Photos can also be useful for creating a library of pop-up projects for historical and reference purposes and for sharing on social media and at library events. The importance of sharing photos of pop-up projects can't be overstated. Sharing, especially on social media, as well as in library promotional materials, photos of patrons and library staff working together on creative projects can be a powerful motivator for others to join in and a catalyst for helping change library culture in an active and engaging way.

MAKE IT YOUR OWN

Once your library has the hang of hosting third-party creative build projects, consider hosting a customized library pop-up makerspace event. Like old-fashioned barn raisings, library events can build community around actual needs, like repairing library furniture, painting murals, enhancing garden areas with benches or artwork, and other basic DIY "home"-style repairs and improvements. Engaging community members in active library improvement projects as part of an over-all plan to build maker culture can create a sense of civic pride and ownership in the library and a new paradigm of the library as an active cultural and creative hub.

Patron projects can also be incorporated into a Made in the Library Fair or special themed library exhibits that highlight creative projects designed. You can also create a photo gallery on your library website to share digitally.

LEARNING ABOUT 3D PRINTERS THROUGH PRACTICAL PRINTING PROJECTS: SEED BOMBS

Once everyone starts getting their minds around "making," the first tool many want to use is a 3D printer. Many libraries now have a 3D printer as part of their facilities, but they use them in different ways. Some libraries have extensive activity programs, while other libraries "exhibit" the machine as a gadget. You could say that the machine is typical of the maker movement: You can make almost anything with it!

Learning about 3D printers can be done in two ways: using a ma-chine-centered focus or learning how to use the machine on the basis of a broader curriculum. While the latter requires more time and energy, using a 3D printer curriculum method has been shown by Paulo Blik-stein, assistant professor of computer science at Stanford University, to lead to better and more valuable results.[8] It also creates the opportunity for a library to develop a sustainable way of integrating a printer by setting up programs or projects.

In this chapter we will look at a specific project used numerous times at a library in Leeuwarden, The Netherlands. The project is about designing and making seed bombs, a seed-filled biodegradable object that makes it possible to sow seeds in hard-to-reach places. This project is actually about sustainability and guerrilla gardening,[9] but the use of the 3D printer is an important part of the program.

Seed bombs typically consist of a mixture of papier-mâché and flow-er seeds. The idea is that these "bombs" are left in places in a town or village that could use some color. Usually, the bombs are kneaded into balls from the traditional mixture of compost and clay, but you can also use the 3D printer to press the mixture into a pretty mold. For example:

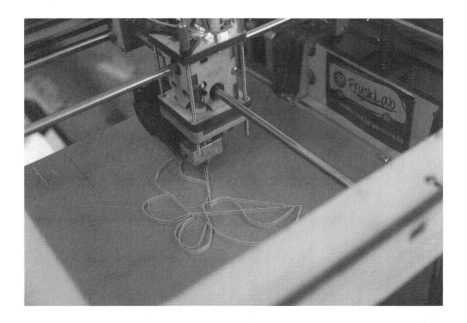

Seed Bomb, *Courtesy of FryskLab.*

You can create a design that depicts the environment or flowers that grow forming your name or have any form you can imagine and create with the 3D printer.

That mold is designed with a design tool like Doodle 3D (perfect for young children) or a program like Tinkercad or Google SketchUp. The activity, which can be carried out perfectly with a group of children who visits the library, begins with a group introduction and encourages collaboration throughout the design process.

Requirements for this workshop (based on twenty participating children, ages eight to fourteen):

- video projector,
- one to three 3D printers,
- Doodle3D,
- tablet (can be any kind of touchscreen device),
- three computers with a Tinkercad account,
- ingredients to make papier-mâché (ten used paperboard egg cartons or paper powder), and
- hand mixers, bowls, and sieves (five each).

Step 1: Understanding Urban Gardening (Duration: 50 minutes)

In this introductory portion of the project, the project leader introduces participants to the idea of urban gardening, explaining that urban gardening and guerrilla gardening are recent movements by community residents to make their environment greener. Besides brightening an urban environment, guerilla gardening has social consequences. People who participate in urban gardening projects will notice that they can affect the environment in which they themselves live and also feel (more) responsible. A short movie, like *Guerilla Gardening—Ninja Girl Spot (with seed bombs)* (https://www.youtube.com/watch?v=rLbe 7l6IWN4), can provide additional information.

Step 2: Short Discussion

After the introduction to urban gardening, ask children about what they've learned and how they feel about the practice. Some examples of conversation starters are:

- Where do they get their food in their home? Supermarket?
- Where are those vegetables growing? Do they cultivate their own vegetables or herbs?
- What is the nearest public piece of green at their home, school, or library?
- Why do people like being urban gardeners?
- What are the solutions they come up with?

Step 3: Project Explanation: What We Need to Know (30 minutes)

Divide children into groups of three to start making seed bombs. Each student in every three-member team has a role: Location Scout, 3D Print Designer, and a Plant or Flower Expert. This means that everyone in the team has his or her own field of expertise, which is discussed and agreed upon by the children themselves.

It is important to realize that no specific knowledge is required for any of the participants. The challenge is to find precisely the role that suits team members best. Children should be guided to work on questions and find solutions together with their fellow group members for the full experience of collaboration.

About the Roles

- *Location Scouts* focus on the social aspects of urban gardening. They consider questions like, "Does it make the environment better, does it strengthen the sense of community, or does it make people aware of where their food comes from?" And most importantly for the project: Do they know a place that may benefit from this in the neighborhood of the library?
- *Designers* consider the form their seed bombs should have. What shape or figure fits the objectives and can help activate people? A 3D printer is used for this part of the project (see Step 6). The design group goes to work with the designing tools and the 3D printer to create the shapes of the seed bombs.
- *Plant Experts* get information about the different seeds. Based on the preferred seed bomb location, they'll need to figure out the most suitable seeds, taking into consideration soil, moisture, and so on.

Step 4: What Are the Challenges? (10 minutes)

The Location Scout for each team is responsible for selecting target locations. They also give the team a name and make appointments to work further on the assignment at or near the chosen location. The Location Scout also collects data and takes photos at the selected location.

The Designer will determine a design that corresponds with the location and will make drawings of selected designs with the Doodle3D to send to the 3D printer.

The Plant Expert will finalize the choice on a combination of seeds on the basis of the chosen location.

Now it's time to start making the seed bombs. This is where the 3D printer comes in.

Step 5: Designing and Printing the Molds (50 minutes)

There are two ways to make designs for this part of the activity. The Netherlands libraries use Doodle3D and Tinkercad, but either one of those options can be used individually, or another design tool can be used.

Requirements

- Doodle3D box,
- computers (three) or tablet,
- 3D printer, and
- Tinkercad account.

Setting Up the 3D Printer

1. Turn on the printer.
2. Make sure there's enough filament (the plastic that is used for printing) available.
3. Check to make sure the filament is unbroken.
4. Make a small test print to make sure the filament is running nicely through the extruder.

Modeling with Doodle3D

Doodle3D consists of a WiFi-Box connected to a tablet or computer. A USB cable connects it to the 3D printer. The box is compatible with a large number of available 3D printers. The beauty of this application is that children can make a drawing on the tablet with their finger or a stylus. Then they press print and the 3D printer starts to work. It's really as easy as that!

Some tips for drawing with Doodle3D:

1. Draw large.
2. If you make a mistake, you go back in time by pressing the OOPS! button.
3. Keep it simple. Ensure that the drawing has plenty of open space in it, and don't fill the spaces with lines or other drawings, which will confuse the 3D printer.

4. Draw as much as possible in one line without releasing the mouse button or stylus or letting your finger off the screen. It is easier for the printer.

5. When you're done and satisfied, the OK button saves the drawing. The drawing can be printed right away, just like sending a document to a regular home office printer.

Modeling with Tinkercad

Complete information and resources are at the Tinkercad website at, as might be expected, Tinkercad.com. All work is done and saved on the web: there's nothing to install onto your computer. You don't need a Tinkercad account to design things, but it's free to set one up. With an account you get to save your work so you can start or finish any kind of project wherever you like. To make things easier, it's helpful to set up one or more Tinkercad accounts in advance. The website 3DVinci includes tutorials and plenty of resources for making the most of this simple but effective 3D drawing tool, as well as other 3D resources.[10]

It's important to note that the molds for the seed bombs can have any desired shape, but there must space for the papier-mâché to be pressed in, so help students design accordingly.

Step 6: Finishing the Seed Bombs (20 minutes)

Each group makes the mixture for seed bombs in which the selected seeds are incorporated. The mixture with the seeds is pressed into the mold to be dried.

To Make the Mixture

Cut the ten paperboard egg cartons into pieces and pour boiling water over them. Let it all soak for one minute, and then mix with a hand mixer. Pour the mixture into the sieve and wait until it thickens enough to be placed on the baking sheet. Press the seeds in it. Dry the mixture out in the sun or near a central heating system until most of the moisture is removed, then press into the 3D molds created by the teams. The seeds mixture will dry further in the molds.

Making Seed Bomb Mixture, *Courtesy of FryskLab.*

Step 7: Presentation (30 minutes)

When complete, invite each group to present their results. In their presentation, they can share their objects and process and show off their seed bombs. And, of course, they finish the project by putting the seed bombs in their chosen location, perhaps around the library.

3D-printed seed bombs are a great practical application of 3D printing technology and a terrific project-based way to learn how to use a 3D printer.

GETTING STARTED WITH ARDUINO: ILLUMINATE YOUR LIBRARY WITH AN LED AMBIENT MOOD LIGHT

Makerspaces often seem to mainly revolve around 3D printing and laser cutting. However, other important key elements of the makerspace are electronics and programming. An application like the Arduino, a simple but high-powered single-board microcontroller, makes this element tangible by combining it with cheap hardware to produce fun

LED Ambient Mood Light

and useful electronics. It's also an excellent way to start tinkering. In *Getting Started with Arduino*,[11] author Massimo Banzi (also the cocreator of Arduino) puts it like this:

> Tinkering is what happens when you try something you don't quite know how to do, guided by whim, imagination, and curiosity. When you tinker, there are no instructions—but there are also no failures, no right or wrong ways of doing things. It's about figuring out how things work and reworking them. Contraptions, machines, wildly mismatched objects working in harmony—this is the stuff of tinkering. Tinkering is, at its most basic, a process that marries play and inquiry.[12]

This is learning by making, the main reason libraries and makerspaces work so well together. The Arduino is a useful, versatile board for the electrical hobbyist, but it takes practice to master. In this section, we translate Arduino to a library workshop setting.

In this workshop, which is suitable for groups as well as individuals, we'll make an LED Ambient Mood Light. The tutorial in this chapter, adapted from an Instructables project,[13] explains how to construct and code an ambient LED light using an Arduino board and some common circuit components. This project mixes a red, green, and blue LED to get a wide range of colors, and the Arduino cycles through them. A paper cover is used to diffuse the light from the discrete LEDs into a more uniform hue.

This project is ideal for adding some mood lighting to a dark room using the Arduino and some common, cheap materials. Participants will go home with a self-made lamp, but you can also ask the participants to illuminate the library.

This tutorial is accessible to anyone starting to work with or interested in using an Arduino board for electrical or art hobby projects. The project takes one to two hours (depending on the experience of the group) and can be executed by a diverse range of participants, ranging from twelve-year-olds to adults.

Step 1: Get Organized

In advance, it is important to determine the resources for offering the workshop. In this case we'll plan the workshop for up to ten people to take place in the library. Because materials have to be purchased in advance, give yourself sufficient time between program registration and the workshop date.

Step 2: Do a Facilities Check

There are two ways to get the materials needed for this activity. Participants can bring their own, or the library can make them available for a fee or provide them for use at no cost through a program grant. Materials for this workshop cost about $35 per person. The Arduino site provides a good guide for various kits and components.[14] Computers necessary for programming the Arduino can be brought in by participants or made available through the library.

For this project the following materials are used:

- Arduino Uno board (older boards should be compatible),
- USB A to USB B connector cable,
- computer with Arduino IDE software,

- Arduino solder-less breadboard shield,
- resistors (330 ohm),
- red, green, and blue LEDs,
- breadboard connector wire,
- white paper,
- scissors, and
- tape.

You will also need the code for this project, which can be found here: http://pastebin.com/1dyWpRuw. The Arduino Software (compiler and IDE) can be found here: http://www.arduino.cc/en/Main/software.

Step 3: Arduino Check

It is advisable to do all the steps that follow along with the group, as well as to encourage participants to help each other as much as possible. If you are using the Arduino for the first time, start by connecting the Arduino to the computer via the USB port. If all goes well you'll see a green LED light up, which is a sign the board is receiving power and is on.

Step 4: LED Circuit Assembly

Now it's time to put together the LED circuit, following the Instructables tutorial. For this process, it is very important to disconnect the Arduino board from its power supply. Then connect the resistors on the breadboard and connect the anodes and cathodes.

If the LEDs fail to light, it's probably because of improper wiring. That's not fatal, just part of the process, and you get to do it all over again for maximum learning. It's important to note that improperly wired circuits can cause the Arduino board to short the USB connection, in which case the USB port may deactivate. If that happens, just restart the computer.

Step 5: Program the Arduino

With the hardware assembled correctly, it's time to program the Arduino. For this step, the software on the Arduino site should be used. The software can be downloaded in advance and made available through the library website, or put it on a USB or SD card for program participants. To familiarize participants with Arduino though, it is advisable to download it directly from the Arduino site (see Step 2) the day of the event. Once the software is downloaded, it must be loaded onto the Arduino board. To do that:

1. Open the Arduino IDE software.[15]
2. Copy and paste the project code into the software.
3. Save and compile the code.
4. Connect the Arduino to the computer via the USB cable.
5. Upload the program to the Arduino.

When all of the above steps go well, the LEDs should light up in seconds and begin fading in and out. When things don't go well, and you don't see the light, consult the troubleshooting guide in the Instructables project guide. When you're back on track, you're ready to build your new lamp!

Step 6: Add a Cover to Diffuse the Light

Once the hardware and software work well, it's time for some old-fashioned cutting and pasting. To make the paper light diffuser, give each participant a rectangular piece of paper. Following the Instructables guide, create a paper cube with one side open. Reinforce the cube's edges with tape, and cut a small hole for the USB that will need to extend through it.

Thanks to the paper cube, the light of the three LEDs will merge into one. Instead of the abrupt LED color transitions, it will result in smooth transitions because the RGB values are blended into one single color.

There are several ways for further experimentation. Depending on the participating group, this may take place in another session in the library, but participants can also do this at home. Step 7 offers an optional segment for this activity.

Properly Configured Arudino

Step 7: Tweak the Project

Finished lamps can be tweaked in various ways. One way is to experiment with different colors of paper or to apply decorations to the lamp cover by drawing on it, adding stickers, or otherwise modifying the diffuser. More adventurous makers may want to tinker with the code. For example, the delay can be adjusted. Using other LED colors naturally leads to different results.

With Arduino it is possible to realize an endless range of creative electronics projects, like illuminating the library. We hope it inspires you to use it as a starting point for many other projects to enrich your offering of library services. Good luck!

HOW TO CREATE A SIMPLE LASER-CUT OBJECT

In public opinion, the 3D printer reigns as the icon of maker culture. However, experience shows that the laser cutter is the real workhorse of a FabLab or makerspace. The device renders objects more quickly than the 3D printer, and it can handle many standard design programs such as Adobe Illustrator or Inkscape. You don't need to master a 3D modeling design tool first to get started. While laser cutters can be expensive, and require physical plant modifications like ventilation systems, their long-term utilitarian value can more than make up for any front-end challenges.

In this project, we will take a photograph and laser cut the image onto wood. This project is part of a library workshop in the mobile FabLab, FryskLab, the Netherlands, in which participants can range from children to adults. Everyone likes to have their picture on wood!

A Look at Laser Cutters

In *The Makerspace Workbench* Adam Kemp describes clearly what a laser cutter is and how it operates: "The laser cutter is a machine that manipulates and focuses a high-power laser beam onto a piece of material following a two-dimensional path generated by a computer. This makes it possible for you to either cut or engrave certain materials with very little waste. The result is a blade-less engraving (raster) and cutting (vector) tool that has virtually limitless application."[16]

The laser lens on a laser cutter works like a magnifying glass to produce a high-powered, amplified beam of focused light that literally carves its way through material. The machine gets very hot and requires a liquid or air cooled system, as well as ventilation. The more powerful the laser, the greater the variety of materials it can be used on, but also the larger space and the better ventilation system you'll need for bigger designs and denser matrials.

Laser cutters require outside ventilation to remove harmful vapors that can be produced while the machine is in operation. Because of this ventilation constraint, direct access to the exterior of a library facility is usually required, though there are also special indoor ventilation systems that can sometimes be utilized.

In addition to sufficient power, ventilation, and space, laser cutters also require a computer for cutting instructions. The computer used for making designs communicates with the laser cutter by using a print driver. Most laser cutters also support offline printing via an SD card. Chapter 3, "Tools and Applications," elaborates on the different kinds of laser cutters and the choices you might want to consider before acquiring one.

Step 1: Get Organized

For this project, you'll need a number of resources and materials. In addition to the laser cutter, you'll need:

- computer with a minimum of 6 GB RAM,
- 2D design software such as Adobe Illustrator, Adobe Photoshop, or CorelDraw,
- fire extinguisher,
- supply of medium-density fiberboard or other material to engrave, and
- digital camera or webcam to make the images you'll be laser cutting.

Step 2: Facilities Check

It's important to make sure everything is in good working order before starting your project.

- Turn on the laser cutter.
- Turn on the cooling system for the laser cutter.
- Make sure that the air vent is working properly.
- Ensure you have a fire extinquisher within reach.

An important note: For safety, as well as accuracy, the laser must always be in focus when in operation. Low-power and out-of-focus laser beams also tend to burn or start fires instead of cutting through materials.

Depending on the machine, focusing can be done automatically or manually. In the case of the particular machine we use, this is a manual process. Focusing the laser is done with the included focus ruler. Please take a look at your manufacturer's laser cutter manual for required steps.

If you are using the software RetinaEngrave for the first time, it is important to go through a few things. For the process of engraving and cutting, the following factors should be checked. Please note these are standard elements of all laser cutting software and not exclusive for the machine we use in this chapter:

Engraving Settings

- Power: The power of the laser corresponds to the depth of the engraving.
- Speed: The faster the tuning of the laser, the more inaccurate it works.
- Image Dithering: This setting determines the degree of contrast of lasered graphics. Each supplier of laser cutters uses its own settings here.
- Resolution: This setting determines how many dots per inch are produced by the laser. A low value will result in a "paler" result because the laser stays shorter on a given place. Please make sure the DPI settings in RetinaEngrave correspond to the image settings.

Cutting Settings

- Frequency: Each material requires a different laser frequency because a laser consists of successive light pulses. Materials such as wood can be cut with a relatively low frequency, as opposed to hard plastics, which need a higher frequency. Each manufacturer has its own presets for different kind of materials.
- Power: The power of the laser corresponds to the depth of the cut. With more power it is possible to cut through thicker materials.
- Speed: Thicker materials ask for the laser to be adjusted to a slower pace.

Step 3: Design!

At FryskLab, the Inkscape design program is used.[17] The lab uses a Full Spectrum Laser,[18] so the software program RetinaEngrave will also be launched (it is also possible to do this later on, but why wait and forget?).

Adobe Illustrator, Adobe Photoshop, or CorelDraw may also be used. After photographing the desired image, it is opened or imported into Inkscape. Because the image will be printed on a wooden or fiberboard with a specific size, the document properties in Inkscape must be resized. After these are adjusted, press print in Inkscape and the coupled laser cutter will show up as one of the available printers.

The print command from Inkscape should automatically open RetinaEngrave. If not, start RetinaEngrave and resume the print job from Inkscape. Within RetinaEngrave a number of specific laser settings can be entered, for example speed and power. It is also possible to adapt the DPI of the printed object. When properly set, the command can be directed toward the cutter.

Step 4: Watching and Smelling the Laser Burn!

Open the machine cover, place the material that needs to be engraved in it, and position the laser head. Then close the machine cover, sit back, and watch and smell the magic happen. Laser-cut wood smells something akin to a campfire, and many find it a pleasant aroma. A wooden board 18.5 cm across takes roughly twenty minutes to finish.

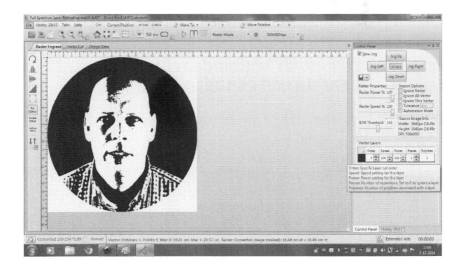

Retina Software Image

Step 5: Enjoy the Wooden Picture!

After the laser has completed the engraving process, the machine cover can be opened and your masterpiece retrieved. Consider making a library gallery of laser-engraved items for all to enjoy!

Laser-Cut Image, *Courtesy of FryskLab.*

HOW TO HOST A *FIRST* ROBOTICS TEAM AT THE LIBRARY: JR. *FIRST* LEGO LEAGUE (JR. FLL)

In addition to making "things" in a makerspace, you can also provide some exciting new program development. Fielding a robotics team at a library is a fun, exciting, and successful way to change up youth programming. *FIRST* is an agile and adaptable K–12 youth STEM education program with a history of library partnership success that not only engages community youth with the library in a new and exciting way, but can reinvigorate staff development and patron interaction as well.

FIRST Things First

The suite of programs includes *FIRST* Robotics Competition (FRC) for students in grades nine through twelve; *FIRST* Tech Challenge (FTC) for grades seven through twelve; *FIRST* LEGO League (FLL) for grades four through eight; and Junior *FIRST* LEGO League (Jr. FLL) for kindergarten through third grade. Key to *FIRST* program success is the emphasis on gracious professionalism. The table on the following pages gives a good at-a-glance look at the different programs and their requirements.

We'll take a step-by-step look at starting a Jr. *FIRST* LEGO League (Jr. FLL) library team here for children ages six to eight, a good age range that's compatible with most library youth programs. Additionally, with the advent of a STAR_Net Jr. FLL Pilot Program[19] in the spring of 2014, there is a wealth of material available to libraries interested in starting Jr. FLL teams that makes rollout even easier.

Step 1: Getting Started: Become Familiar with Jr. *FIRST* LEGO League

The best way to learn the Jr. FLL ropes is the Jr. FLL website at http://www.juniorfirstlegoleague.org. In a nutshell, Jr. FLL is a hands-on program designed to pique young children's interest and curiosity in science and technology. With guidance from adult coaches and under the ethos of Jr. FLL Core Values, team members work with LEGO elements and motorized parts to illustrate potential solutions to a real-world challenge. There is also a "research" component to exercise other aspects of critical thinking and imagination.

Start-up costs are about $300 per team, which includes the annual $50 registration fee, the reusable base kit, and consumables like art supplies. Annual Challenges have a different theme each year and consist of two main parts: the LEGO Model and the Show Me Poster. Teams consist of two to six children, with support from at least two adults. During the season the team will:

- conduct research about the current Challenge theme;
- build a LEGO Model based on the Challenge instructions that features both a simple machine and a motorized part; and

Table 5.1.

Program	Jr. FLL	FLL	FTC	FRC
Age range/grade	Ages 6–9	Ages 9–14	Grades 7–12	Grades 9–12
Size of team	5–6 children	10 max.	15 max.	10+
Size of robot	No robot, LEGO model	16" sq. using LEGO Mindstorms kit	18" sq. , can be up to 30+ lbs., built with TETRIX aluminum and other materials	Up to 120 lbs. of metal, gears, electronics, pneumatics, and more
Est. cost*	$210 U.S.—reusable kit, annual registration fee $50	$500 U.S.—reusable kit, annual reg. fee $225, plus $75 field setup kit, with competition fees ranging from $25–$50; community registration option available	$750 U.S.—reusable kit, with LEGO Mindstorms and Wi-Fi module; annual reg. fee $275, plus competition fees ranging from $25–$100	$6500 rookie team, $5000 veteran team; includes kit of parts and registration in 1 event; $5000 each additional event
Season	Nov.–June	Sept.–January	Sept.–January	6 weeks, Jan.–Feb.
Tools needed	None	None	Hand tools, some power tools	Hand tools, power tools, machine shop
Build space req.	Standard meeting room	Standard meeting room/ garage	Classroom size	Classroom plus machine shop
# of meetings	Varies on group and complexity of project solutions—anywhere from 3 to 10 one- to two-hour meetings	Weekly three-to four-hour meetings for 8 to 12 weeks or more	Weekly four- to six-hour meetings for 8 to 12 weeks or more	2–3/week or more, for 6–8 hours per meeting—teams may invest up to 30 hrs+ per week in season
# of coaches	2	2	2–4	2–6

# of events	I or 2 as desired	I–3 plus a regional event and maybe a state championship— community option allows for in-house events instead	3–6 events, depending on area, a state championship, and possibly a "super-regional" championship	Usually one 4-day regional event, but some teams may opt for a second or third event

*Prices current as of March 2015. Visit USFIRST.org for updated information. Costs do not include competition travel expenses or extra parts or other potential related costs.

- display their findings on a Show Me Poster.

Rather than participate in "competitions," the Jr. FLL experience culminates in an "Expo," a tradeshow-like experience where teams share their creations and their research with adult judges. The Jr. FLL season typically lasts six to eight weeks, though some teams may run longer, and libraries can cultivate a Jr. FLL "club" experience that runs year round.

Step 2: Identify Your Champions

There should be at least two library staff willing to be lead contacts for the library program, as well as two parent/mentors per team to ensure team sustainability and maximum program support. Once you have committed adult support, you can begin promoting your program. Staff running the program should expect about one to two hours a week of preparation and planning time, and a once-a-week, hour-long team meeting with students. Parents/mentors should plan on at least one hour a week of volunteer time during meetings.

Step 3: Get Organized

Jr. FLL is intended to be a high-impact, but low-key, low-stress experience for students and adults. Being organized is an important aspect of an enjoyable experience for all involved, so the more front-end work you can do, the better.

Start by deciding whether you want to host one team of five to six students or a couple or three teams, and make sure you have sufficient adult support for your program. Then:

- Create a project timeline that works for you, your coaches, and your teams, planning backward from the date you want to hold your Expo. In the beginning teams may only meet once a week, but you may want to meet twice a week nearer to the Expo date.
- Identify a meeting space. For small children, especially, it's good to have the same meeting space every week to help establish routine and familiarity. Make sure you have storage space for backpacks and clothing items, as well as for Jr. FLL materials. You'll also need comfortable work space for drawing and building with the LEGOs.
- Consider meeting days and times. Decide on a specific day and time for team meetings in advance of promoting your program, or you can wait until your teams are filled to figure out what schedule works best for everyone participating, though even then you'll want to have some set dates for people to choose from to prevent having to field a dozen different requests.
- Secure supplies. You'll need writing and drawing tools, poster board, and storage bins for LEGO materials.

Step 4: Promote Your Program

Once you have your volunteers in place, and your program schedule, start recruiting! Create a promotional flyer and keep a Jr. FLL sign-up sheet in your children's area and online. Be clear on the number of slots available. If you have five coaches, then you can support up to thirty children in your program. If you have only two coaches, then up to twelve children can sign up.

Your sign-up sheet should include space for child's name and age and parent's name and phone number. Children's ages are important because, depending on the number of teams being created, youth can be kept in closer age groups if needed.

You can also include on the promo flyer the chosen meeting day and time for team meetings, or a couple of meeting options for registrants to choose from, which will provide good insight into trends in availability.

Make sure to include only dates that work best for your library, coaches, and volunteers.

Step 5: Create Your Team

There is no right or wrong way to create a team. If you only want to field one team, cap registration at six students. If you feel comfortable fielding more than one team, plan registration accordingly. Once you have your coaches and children signed up, make sure each team has at least two adult coaches.

Set meeting expectations early, and codify clearly for students and adults. For *FIRST* LEGO League and *FIRST* Tech Challenge teams, it's good to have a team handbook, meeting guidelines, and parent-student-coach agreements. For Jr. FLL, posting a simple set of meeting guidelines (take turns talking, play nice, etc.) and the Jr. FLL Core Values should do the trick.

Step 6: Register Your Team

To register a team, go to USFIRST.org, select Jr. FLL, and follow the directions from there to register your team or teams in "TIMS," the Team Information Management System, as follows:

1. Create a New User.
2. Click the button *Add New Team*. You will receive a temporary team number through the e-mail you originally signed up with. After payment is received, a permanent four-digit team number will be assigned.
3. Click *Complete Profile* for your temporary team, which will bring you to a Team Summary page where all the relevant information can be entered now or completed later.

After receiving your four-digit team number, access to a variety of areas will become available. Click the Edit/View button to access registered and paid teams and update information as needed. You'll also be able to order materials, Challenge information, and resources and access the Online Showcase and private Jr. FLL Forum where you can connect with other coaches, share resources, and get help.

Step 7: Meet and Create!

The Jr. FLL season is six to eight weeks long, and there are two components to the program experience: The Model and the Show Me Poster.

- The Model: For Jr. FLL, students will be building, over the course of their season, a Model out of LEGO® parts that is related to the season theme, fits within a 15-inch x 15-inch footprint, and has at least one motorized piece. Part of the model includes a simple machine that uses LEGO ramps, levers, pulleys, gears, wheels and axles, screws, or wedges.
- Show Me Poster: Students also create a "Show Me" tri-fold poster that describes, with words, photos, and drawings, what they learned during their Challenge research; describes their Model and simple machine; and talks about their team.

Here is a sample schedule for meetings:

- Housekeeping/Admin: 10 minutes. Start with a project timeline, planning backward from the first competition date, and help team members set milestone dates. During the administrative portion of each meeting, do a status check and set reasonable team goals for that day. This is the time to field most questions, concerns, and ideas.
- Team Building: 10 minutes. Do a short team-building exercise— building a marshmallow and toothpick structure or playing some active game to get the wiggles out.
- Research: 20 minutes. The Jr. FLL manual provides comprehensive information about the research project. Use this time to use some simple research tools or maybe have a guest speaker or presenter who can give team members some insights and ideas about their topic.
- Model Building: Depending on ages, figure 30 minutes to 45 minutes. This is the part the kids typically really want to do. Help guide collaboration and exploration as children design to the theme and work on their simple machine.
- Wrap Up: 15 minutes. This is the time to teach responsible use of library facilities (and any facilities, really) and respect for those who will use spaces after the students. Making this a routine part

of every meeting helps keep materials accounted for and spaces organized and clean.

Step 8: Host an Expo

The Jr. FLL Expo is a noncompetitive event with no specific awards but recognizing participation of all teams. Library Jr. FLL Expos provide a great opportunity to engage not only students and their families, but library patrons in a celebratory showcase of youth achievement. A typical Expo lasts approximately two to four hours. Volunteer Reviewers visit with each team, check out team-built Models, and ask questions. The idea is to give children an opportunity to share what they've created in a celebratory environment and to give them a chance to see what other teams have done.

Step 9: Celebrate!

Have an end-of-season party. Make a community event of it, and showcase students and their season achievements with Friends and patrons in a library-wide event. Run videos from the Expo, display student work and any trophies that may have been won, and let the students share their energy and enthusiasm with guests. This is a great way to recruit new team members and volunteers for the next season and get everyone excited about the library as a place of energy and creative action.

HANDS-ON ENGAGEMENT FOR SENIOR MAKERS: SQUISHY CIRCUITS

Tinkering with 3D printers and electronics isn't just for younger folks. Libraries are uniquely positioned to provide opportunities for an often underserved population of creative and productive individuals: senior makers. Older library patrons tend to hold libraries in particularly high esteem. According to a 2011 Harris Poll on American Libraries, "Senior citizens (38 percent) are significantly more likely than other older adults (25 percent of those aged 55 to 64) to rank the benefits of the public library at the top of the list of tax-supported services."

They are also more likely to be donors. The Dorothy Lumley Melrose Center for Technology, Innovation and Creativity at Orlando Public Library was made possible by a $1 million donation from an elder patron's endowment.

While most makerspaces cater to a younger crowd, libraries have a built-in fan base among those sixty and older and can be a safe and welcoming haven for older patrons looking to improve digital literacy, refresh craft and trade skills, and explore twenty-first-century tools like 3D printers and Arduinos.

Kate Farina, a public programs coordinator in San Diego, has done some interesting work in the field, trying to develop suitable electronics toolkits for senior citizens.[20] Farina believes that "people who are used to, literally, doing things 'by hand' (especially hand crafts or hobby projects) will be better able to understand computing basics through making physical programmable objects, as opposed to interactions that are only screen-and-software-based. Physical computing is a really great blend of creative expression and ingenuity and problem solving and practical application."

"Squishy Circuits," developed by the University of St. Thomas (St. Paul, Minnesota), can provide an accessible and understandable delivery platform for new skills development and knowledge acquisition in a familiar package, as well as being adaptable to various degrees of manual dexterity and just plain fun![21] Soft clay circuits are also much easier for older fingers to handle than the smaller SparkFun kits or even littleBits. So get cooking with some electronic dough and see what amazing electronic art your senior makers will create.

Step 1: Senior Volunteer Engagement

Before launching into a clay-based electronics class, it's a good idea to take the pulse of your senior patrons, so to speak. An informal poll of older library volunteers will probably turn up some artsy individuals who would enjoy trying their hand at Squishy Circuits and could then act as program assistants for a patron class. Older library volunteers can then act as a conduit to the community of senior library patrons.

Step 2: Make Some Dough: Conductive and Insulating Dough

This project requires two different kinds of dough: conductive dough and insulating dough. The recipes are pretty basic—flour, water, and salt and lemon juice for the conductive dough, and sugar for the insulating dough—and can be found online at http://courseweb.stthomas.edu/apthomas/SquishyCircuits/howTo.htm. The conductive dough has to be made on a stovetop, so project prep will probably require an off-site location. But the dough can be stored in plastic containers and will keep for a few days.

Step 3: Assemble Squishy Circuits Kits

In addition to the two types of dough, for a basic session you'll also need:

- LEDs,
- 9-volt battery clips,
- 9-volt batteries, and
- mini storage boxes.

Create individual kits of about a dozen LEDs, a 9-volt battery clip, and a battery in each mini storage box. Now you can provide each participant, or small teams of three to four, with a Squishy Circuits build kit that includes a container of conductive dough, a container of insulating dough, and a little box of components.

Step 4: Host a Squishy Circuits Staff Play Date

Tinkering with Squishy Circuits isn't rocket science, but there's a bit of a learning curve to working with the stuff, and for the most successful patron engagement session it's best to have staff and volunteers who have worked with the material themselves. So throw a play date, and invite those senior volunteers and programming staff to come play with clay.

Cover some tables with craft paper and, depending on the number of participants, supply each person or small team of two to four people with Squishy Circuits Kits and have at it.

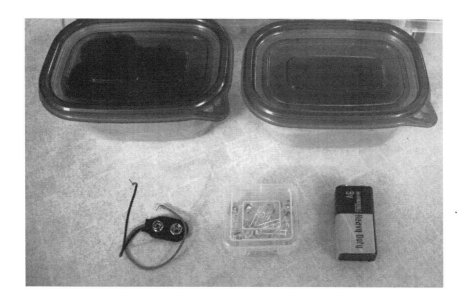

Squishy Circuits Project Kits

Step 5: Oreo Power: Making a Simple Circuit

This is a very simple project to illustrate how electricity flows in a circuit and can be used in the creation of other projects. Here are the basics: Electricity takes the path of least resistance. So if two conductive pieces of clay attached to battery leads are touching, and you stick an LED on them, the LED won't light up because the electricity just flows between the dough pieces, bypassing the LED. That's a short circuit.

If, however, you separate the two conductive pieces of dough, or put an insulating piece of dough before them (creating an Oreo cookie effect), and then attach an LED wire to each piece of conductive dough, the LED will light up.

Make sure the polarity on your LEDs is correct, with the longer, positive lead attached to the side with the red battery wire, and the shorter, negative lead going to the side with the black wire. There must be dough between the LED and battery terminals to prevent the LED from burning out.

Oreo Circuit

Step 6: It's a Parallel Universe

Once everyone has the hang of the simple Oreo circuit, start mixing it up with series and parallel circuits. Series circuits are just a bunch of "Oreo cookies" stacked side by side, or a long "snake" of insulating dough between two walls of conductive dough. You'll find that the longer you make your series, the dimmer the LEDs will get until they don't light at all, because there's less electricity available down the line.

Parallel circuits, however, allow more paths for electricity to flow. Here, all you need is a bigger Oreo setup, with LEDs stacked along the insulating dough and wired in parallel to the battery, as the single LED was. Now if one LED burns out or is removed, the others continue burning as brightly—in essence, a modern Christmas light string.

With these basic principles, makers can now create a variety of electronic sculptures using the two different kinds of dough, LEDs, and small motors.

Step 7: Host a Senior Maker Party!

An hour session of tinkering with Squishy Circuits should make most staff and volunteers sufficiently comfortable with the material to share the fun with senior patrons at a Senior Maker Party. Invite older patrons to an afternoon of music, snacks, and refreshments and provide a short presentation on creative programming and the "maker" experience, then break out the Squishy Circuits Kits.

Keep explanations short and sweet. Many older patrons may already have enough basic electronics know-how to just plunge in and play. Be sure to tell participants they can't hurt anything and there's no "wrong" way to work with the clay and circuits.

Run everyone through the simple Oreo cookie circuit and then step back. You'll probably be surprised and delighted with the amazing things people come up with as they explore different configurations of the clay and LEDs.

Other fun projects for senior makers include using MaKey MaKey kits, creating knitted circuits, building moisture sensors for indoor plants, and more.

CREATING AN ENTREPRENEURSHIP CENTER

Entrepreneurship is part and parcel of maker culture. The things people create, from physical products to apps, to fine crafts and art and inventions, are all potentially marketable items that can provide economic well-being for the producers of those items.

Libraries are well positioned to support entrepreneurial growth and development in their communities, with everything from meeting space, to opportunities for training, consultation, and general small business support in collaboration with government small business resource providers and community partners. In "What Is Entrepreneurial Librarianship?" Stephanie Prato says librarians can be essential resources to entrepreneurs and start-ups: "These librarians understand that knowing how to conduct effective research, including topics like trademark/copyright laws and market research, in addition to the specific domain areas of the product or service being produced is essential to a successful business venture."[22]

In fact, Prato says, as champions of intellectual freedom, providing equal access to information and platforms for democratic conversation, librarians are already social entrepreneurs, and libraries are natural places for entrepreneurial support and development. Creating a formal center for business support in your library will not only enhance services provided to patrons, but also establish your library as an integral component of economic development in your community to the long-term benefit of both your community and your library.

Step 1: Evaluate Your Facility

An Entrepreneurship Center doesn't have to have a big footprint. An existing meeting or study room will do, especially if you're going to have specific set hours or days of the week that the center is open. If you plan on having the space available for work or consultation services during regular library hours, you'll need some dedicated space, and staff, that can accommodate traffic throughout the day.

Ideally, you'll also want:

- high-speed Wi-Fi for easy access to online resources and tools,
- white boards/smart boards or whiteboard walls for brainstorming and capturing ideas,
- projector and screen, or flat-screen monitor,
- conference table for four to eight people or more, with sufficient seating, and
- two or three work stations able to accommodate one to three people each, with computer and mobile device charging stations.

Depending on your library's facilities arrangements, you may even be able to consider "coworking" space. Coworking is a flexible, shared working environment where people from different companies or small businesses can work simultaneously, in shared office space, eliminating the expense of full-scale, dedicated offices.

In Arizona, a partnership between Arizona State University and the Scottsdale Public Library System has resulted in the Civic Center Library EUREKA coworking space,[23] where local small business owners and innovators have access to work space while also receiving mentorship, advice, and some training, online and in the library. If your library has sufficient space, being able to offer "office hours" for small independent businesses can provide a valuable community resource.

Step 2: Conduct a Community Partner Inventory

Good community partners are key to any successful Entrepreneurship Center. Contact your local Small Business Administration (SBA) center and talk to them about your efforts in order to see what organizations might be able to provide the best support in your area. Also reach out to local academic institutions, which often have business development centers of their own to support their academic community. Another resource is your county or city economic development office, which would probably welcome more community support.

In Pasco County, Florida, Pasco County Libraries are part of the Pasco Enterprise Network, a group of organizations that includes local Chambers of Commerce, the Pasco Economic Development Council (PEDC), area colleges, and business advisory groups committed to fostering economic development.[24] Working with PEDC, the library system has launched SizeUp for Local Business Intelligence (SizeUp LBI), a market research and performance benchmarking tool for business development, and a partnership with a municipal library in the county is exploring the development of a FabLab to be managed by the library in a county business incubator.

Other potential partners include:

- SCORE (formerly known as Service Corps of Retired Executives), a nonprofit association composed of more than thirteen thousand volunteer business counselors throughout the United States who are trained to serve as counselors, advisors, and mentors to aspiring entrepreneurs and business owners. Services are offered at no fee as a community service.
- Small Business Development Center, a collaboration of the Small Business Administration (SBA), federal funds, state and local governments, and private sector resources.
- TiE—The Indus Entrepreneurs, begun by Indian business leaders in California in 1992—is a nonprofit dedicated to fostering entrepreneurship through mentoring, networking, education, incubating, and funding. While Indian in origin, the group is inclu-

sive by nature and welcomes opportunities to support entrepreneurship in communities everywhere.

- Etsy's Craft Entrepreneurship Program (http://craft entrepreneurship.com), a community program of the popular online craft store where individual artisans and crafters sell their wares, is composed of self-organized groups of Etsy members who come together to collaborate, teach, and learn from one another.
- VentureLab, and similar youth entrepreneurship programs, is a hands-on innovation and entrepreneurship program that encourages innovation and entrepreneurship through inspiration, experiential learning, and mentorship.

Search on "entrepreneurship" on your local MeetUp site to find additional potential partners.

Connecting with good partners will not only enhance the services you can provide with your Entrepreneurship Center, it can open up sponsorship opportunities through naming rights and create a greater sense of community ownership that can help make your center a point of civic pride.

Step 3: Conduct a Patron Inventory

What's the economic landscape in your community? Hold some discovery sessions (see chapter 2) with patrons to get a real-time picture of needs and interests. It won't be of much use to provide business support for web developers if patron interests are more aligned with arts or construction.

Is your patron population mostly young adults or do you serve a retiree community? You can provide the best support if you understand the people you're trying to support.

Step 4: Identify Scope of Services and Set Clear Goals

There's no need to try to be all things to all people. Take the time to get a feel for what works best with your Entrepreneurship Center and to set out clear expectations both for partners and for patrons. Unless you've got a big facility, plenty of support, and strong community partnerships, the most likely scenario is that people with small business needs will be able to come to your library once or twice a week to get basic business guidance.

They'll meet with business development counselors and reference librarians to get the facts on starting and maintaining a business, different types of business models, and help filing paperwork and understanding finances. More robust programs may be able to provide patent help and more advanced business development support.

Whatever level of support you're able to provide, lay it out clearly in flyers, on your website and on-site, with good signage to identify your Entrepreneurship Center spaces, a line-up of workshops, and communications support in place. People looking for business support have a lot of questions, so having some assigned staff is helpful.

Have a data-gathering process in place, too. You'll want to be able to collect some pre- and post-center usage data and monitor the effectiveness of the center over time. Being able to document the success of your Entrepreneurship Center can lead to greater funding support, more community engagement, and more partner involvement. Understanding what isn't working can save you time, money, and staff and keep you from spinning your wheels to provide business support that isn't needed or doesn't work.

Based on your facilities availability, staff capabilities, and patron and community needs, you'll be able to decide how often and how long you're open, what types of workshops to offer, and what kind of counseling services should be available.

Step 5: Launch Your Entrepreneurship Center!

Consider starting with some specifically targeted programs that have very clear starting and ending periods, like a VentureLabs program for youth or an Etsy Craft Entrepreneurship program, similar to the one run by the Public Library of Chattanooga, Tennessee, which partnered with local Etsy sellers to provide a free month-long "craft entrepreneurship" training program.[25] The program uses Etsy's online sales platform in a "real world learning lab" that helped participants "learn basic online business skills, such as pricing, accounting, product photography and marketing."

Holding weekly SBA or SCORE workshops is also an effective way to engage people with the Entrepreneurship Center. Holding a multiweek course or holding a series of workshops is a good way to introduce people to the center and raise its visibility. From there, add business counseling availability to gauge interest and usage and build out your entrepreneurship services.

Create a companion Small Business Resource collection of related books, DVDs, and instructional materials that can be housed in or near your Entrepreneurship Center, along with a kiosk of informational material provided by partners and local agencies to complete your support center.

Step 6: Celebrate Entrepreneurship with a Small Business Day Event

After your first round or two of workshops and programs, invite community partners, patrons, and the immediate community to a Small Business Day Celebration. Showcase local businesses and products, highlight Entrepreneurship Center partners, and invite local civic and economic development leaders to join in.

A library-based Entrepreneurship Center can be a true community gem, providing an accessible and affordable way to helping revitalize neighborhoods, build economic development, and improve the lives and well-being of residents and their families.

HOSTING A HACKATHON, BUILDING A CODING COMMUNITY

A "hackathon," also known as a Hack Day or Hack Fest, is a community event designed to engage those involved in software and, sometimes, hardware development, along with an often diverse crowd of creative individuals with interests in everything from graphic design to gaming. Hackathons can be themed, or just provide opportunities for people with coding and development interests to gather and create together. Most hackathons are informal get-togethers. Others are part of nationally synchronized events like National Day of Civic Hacking, which takes place in the summer.

With groups like Code for America, there can also be a civic engagement aspect to a hackathon. Code for America is a national network of
civic-minded volunteers who contribute their skills toward using the
web as a platform for local government and community service, making
an association with the library a perfect fit.

A great way to start building a coding community is to host a hackathon. Hosting a hackathon at a library will bring a lot of interesting, and
interested, individuals to your facility, raising awareness of the mutually
beneficial relationship between coders and the library. So let's look at
how to host a hackathon, and then we'll look at how to keep the coders.

Step 1: Do a Facilities Check

Hackathons don't require a lot in the way of physical resources beyond
tables and chairs, comfortable environment, and access to power. But
they do have a lot of technical requirements, which the Hackday Manifesto outlines in great detail at http://hackdaymanifesto.com/. Read it in
its entirety on the website, since we'll only touch on some of the most
fundamental needs here. These include:

- reliable, easily accessible Wi-Fi with good Wi-Fi security—keeping in mind that the more Wi-Fi users you have, the less reliable
  most Wi-Fi can be;
- open and accessible system with minimal firewalls;
- Internet backup in case of power failures;
- Ethernet availability, preferably with extra cables;
- access to power at the rate of 1.5 power sockets for every seat;
- audio/video support for any presentations; and
- access to local civic data sets and APIs (Application Program
  Interfaces—the sets of routines, protocols, and tools needed for
  building software applications).

A single large meeting space is ideal, but several small spaces can work
as well. Food and beverages go hand in hand with long coding and
development sessions, so plan accordingly.

Step 2: Decide on a Format and Goals

You can host a half-day hackathon with a particular goal, which in many libraries that host hackathons can focus on things like writing a library app or improving Online Patron Access (OPAC) or other services for patrons. Or you can host a multiday event with or without a theme. Some events award prizes. Others are just opportunities to work together on projects but have no clearly defined "winners." If you do prizes, they should be awarded to teams rather than individuals, so make sure they're appropriate. Either way, you still need objectives, some takeaway for the end of the day or the end of the weekend.

You also need to take food into consideration—programming and eating tend to go hand in hand (or perhaps, hand to mouth). Will you be serving full meals or just snack items? Will there be workshops? Some events are training opportunities as well, providing opportunities to learn about different APIs or development methodologies, in which case you'll need to engage workshop leaders, which should not be too hard if you start recruiting participants and event partners early (see Step 4).

Step 3: Set Clear Rules of Conduct and Participation

A hackathon without some guidelines can be a frustrating experience for organizers as well as participants. Event guidelines should include the mission of the event, hours, limits of hardware or software, and the data sources that participants will have access to during the event. Participants should receive a copy of the guidelines when they register, and they should be reviewed the day of the event at the hackathon kickoff.

Step 4: Recruit Attendees Early

The coding community is just that, a community that needs time to become aware of an upcoming event and values opportunities to be part of making it happen. Once you have an idea of your space and focus, start reaching out via social media or with sign-up sheets at your library. Hosting a pre-event meet-up will help build out the event agenda, as well as generate buzz and fresh ideas from stakeholders.

Engaging the coding community early results in better participation and a sense of ownership and commitment, which will help make the event a real success. It's important to reach out to the right groups to connect with the types of individuals most likely to attend a hackathon. So take stock of coding organizations like CoderDojo, organized meetups of various programming user groups, and professional associations like the IEEE (Institute of Electrical and Electronics Engineers) and others. The more people you can bring into the early planning stages, the better, since only about 60 percent of event registrants typically attend—common across many events.

Another benefit to early recruitment is the potential to develop new and possibly long-term relationships with groups that might want to consider meeting more regularly at the library and who might be able to provide classes and programming at later dates.

Step 5: Set Agenda and Registration

Pick a day and time and develop an event schedule, with break times or meal times scheduled in. Make sure everyone you've spoken with in the early planning stages is aware of registration information and deadlines. Having a flyer with all the relevant information on it to distribute to your organizing partner groups will help ensure extensive outreach to the relevant community.

Multiday hackathons are often held on weekends. Some events might be more successful as a weekday afternoon event. Consider work schedules, and if you're doing a weekend event, look at other possible competing events—though for coders and the like, there probably won't be many other competitive events.

Step 6: Promote

Promoting the event creates the energy that makes it exciting for participants and raises library visibility in the tech community. If you can have a free-standing webpage for the event, that's ideal. But promoting via the usual library social media channels, with flyers and news, is also effective.

If your event is part of a bigger one, like the National Day of Civic Hacking, it's even easier to surf the tide of national promotion, leveraging bigger organizations' social media and website resources.

Step 7: Hackathon Day

The schedule for the day should be available before the event and reviewed at the start of the event day or weekend. A typical two-day event schedule looks something like this:

Saturday, 9 a.m.: Check In—Meet and Greet

People who know each other may form immediate affinity groups that become teams, and even strangers just meeting for the first time can usually pair up pretty easily. Teams can consist of a couple of people or several, with the sense of community inherent in most hack groups lending itself to collaboration without much guidance. Coffee and bagels or donuts can be effective ice breakers.

9:30 a.m.: Welcome and Event Overview

If the event is themed around some central challenge like transportation or communications, set the challenge out at this time. If the event is more user led, where teams are coming up with their own ideas or solutions to problems they'd like to address, then proceed right to an event overview, reviewing the schedule and event guidelines.

11 a.m.: Scrum Time!

Get out of the way while teams brainstorm ideas and strategize their approaches. Allow at least an hour.

Noon: Lunch

1:00 p.m.–5 p.m.: Team Project Resumes

This is also a good time for workshops, if any will be provided. Otherwise, teams can resume brainstorming or begin work on their projects. Keep snacks and refreshments at hand throughout the day.

5 p.m.: Wrap Up Day One

Sunday, 10 a.m.: Hacking Resumes

12:30 p.m.: Lunch

1:30 p.m.–2:30 p.m.: Hacking Stops; Projects Submitted

It's fairly standard practice, with or without judging or prizes, to have a stopping point midday, at which point teams will prepare their "pitches" for their projects to share with one another.

3 p.m.: Project Pitches

Have a projector and screen that teams can use to showcase their work. Some projects won't be finished, which is fine. Teams can still talk about their effort and goals.

4:30 p.m.: Sum Up

If the group as a whole is selecting a winner, make awards at this time, or just call it a fun weekend and celebrate with some pizza. The whole point of a hackathon is to provide an opportunity for networking and collaboration, with bonus points for the development of a useful app, website, or digital tool that provides a solution to an identified problem. If most participants can come out of the event with a sense of camaraderie and some new knowledge, the event has been a resounding success.

Step 8: Stay Connected

The best hackathons are a starting point, not just for participants, but for the library, helping establish a new gathering place for coders, developers, and other technical groups. After the hackathon, reach out to participants with regular opportunities for meet-ups and networking, and invite individuals and groups, like CoderDojo and Code for America, to make use of the library for their events and programs. It's also a good idea to archive hackathon projects and results on your library's website or blog so participants can enjoy some recognition and their projects can get continued use.

The library is uniquely positioned not just as a community gathering place, put as a vital resource for data access and research resources, two vital tools for developers interested in addressing social and civic needs, and two vital ways the library can support a robust programmers' community that will serve not only the community, but the library as well.

NOTES

1. "Instructables—DIY How to Make Instructions," Instructables.com. http://www.instructables.com (accessed June 27, 2014).

2. "Make It @ Your Library," http://makeitatyourlibrary.org.

3. "Tools and Space Descriptions," Make It @ Your Library, http://makeitatyourlibrary.org/node/51#.U7Cx2_ldV8E (accessed June 27, 2014).

4. "Hack a Day," Hackaday Projects, http://hackaday.io/projects (accessed July 7, 2014).

5. "Make: Projects," *Make:*, http://makezine.com/projects/ (accessed July 7, 2014).

6. "Red Bull Creation," Red Bull, http://creation.redbullusa.com/about/ (accessed July 7, 2014).

7. littleBits, http://littlebits.cc/new_home (accessed July 7, 2014).

8. Paulo Blikstein, "Digital Fabrication and 'Making' in Education: The Democratization of Invention," in *FabLab: Of Machines, Makers and Inventors*, ed. J. Walter-Herrmann and C. Büching (Bielefeld: Transcript Publishers, 2013).

9. "Guerrilla Gardening Seed Bomb Guide," http://www.guerrilla gardening.org/ggseedbombs.html (accessed November 30, 2014).

10. Bonnie Roskes, "Getting Started in Tinkercad," 3DVinci, http://www. 3dvinci.net/PDFs/GettingStartedInTinkercad.pdf (accessed November 30, 2104).

11. Massimo Banzi, *Getting Started with Arduino*, 2nd ed. (San Francisco: Maker Media, 2011).

12. "Tinkering: All Summer at the Exploratorium," Exploratorium, http://www.exploratorium.edu/tinkering (accessed November 30, 2014).

13. "How to Make an LED Ambient Mood Light: A Beginner Tutorial," Instructables.com, January 1, 2011, http://www.instructables.com/id/How-to-Make-an-LED-Ambient-Mood-Light-A-Beginner- (accessed November 30, 2014).

14. "Arduino—Buy." Arduino, http://www.arduino.cc/en/Main/Buy (accessed November 30, 2014).

15. "Arduino—Software." Arduino, http://www.arduino.cc/en/Main/software (accessed November 30, 2014).

16. Adam Kemp, *The Makerspace Workbench: Tools, Technologies, and Techniques for Making* (Sebastopol, CA: Maker Media, 2013).

17. Inkscape, http://www.inkscape.org/ (accessed December 4, 2014).

18. Full Spectrum Laser, http://fslaser.com/ (accessed December 4, 2014).

19. Anne Holland, "STAR Library Education Network (STAR_Net) and Junior FIRST® LEGO® (Jr.FLL®) Grant Opportunity—Deadline April 4, 2014," New Jersey State Library, January 1, 2014, http://www.njstatelib.org/event/star_library_education_network_star_net_and_junior/ (accessed September 20, 2014).

20. Kate Farina, "Senior Citizens Can Build Gadgets: Physical Computing Kits for Lifelong Learning," http://www.katefarina.com/portfolio-item/senior-citizens-can-build-gadgets-physical-computing-kits-for-lifelong-learning/ (accessed September 10, 2014).

21. AnnMarie Thomas, "Welcome to the Squishy Circuits Project Page," Squishy Circuits, http://courseweb.stthomas.edu/apthomas/SquishyCircuits/index.htm (accessed September 10, 2014).

22. Stephanie Prato, "What Is Entrepreneurial Librarianship?" Syracuse University School of Information Studies, June 5, 2013, http://infospace.ischool.syr.edu/2013/06/05/what-is-entrepreneurial-librarianship (accessed December 11, 2014).

23. "EUREKA—ASU and Arizona Libraries Collaborate to Offer Co-Working Spaces and Entrepreneurship Support Through New Alexandria Network," University Economic Development Association, http://universityeda.org/eureka-asu-and-arizona-libraries-collaborate-to-offer-co-working-spaces-and-entrepreneurship-support-through-new-alexandria-network/ (accessed December 11, 2014).

24. "Libraries Find a New Role in Economic Development," GIS Planning, http://www.gisplanning.com/_blog/GIS_Planning_Blog/post/libraries-find-a-new-role-in-economic-development/ (accessed December 11, 2014).

25. Chloé Morrison, "Library Partners with Etsy for New Craft Entrepreneurship Program," Nooga.com, October 3, 2014, http://www.nooga.com/167988/library-partners-with-etsy-for-new-craft-entrepreneurship-program/ (accessed December 11, 2014).

6

TIPS AND TRICKS

MAKING THE BEST OF THINGS: BEST PRACTICES FOR CREATING AGILE AND ENDURING LIBRARY MAKERSPACES

Congratulations! If you've gotten this far, you're hopefully invested in both the spirit and intent of library makerspaces. There's clearly a lot of moving parts to developing creative space and programming in the library. But we hope it's clear by now, as well, that the rewards for libraries that step out into this fresh new territory are many, rich, and varied. Changing up space and programming to accommodate the creative culture is good for patrons, for libraries, and for the communities they serve.

To that end, we offer a collection of tips and tricks and best practices that we hope will make implementation of makerspaces, FabLabs, and creative programming in your library a little easier. There's no substitute for experience, of course, and your mileage may vary, but the following recommendations come courtesy of our own experience, and others', to aid you on your own makerspace journey.

FOCUS ON PEOPLE, NOT TECHNOLOGY

Don't let shiny tech distract you: Makerspaces are about people, not technology. Technology is a tool, a means to an end, not the end itself. Think about why you want to have a makerspace in the first place.

For many libraries, the impetus for creative space and programming is part of an overall desire to better engage the immediate community, to increase patronage or improve patron services and experiences. All those things are about people, not technology. The success of your space will depend on the people who use it, run it, volunteer in it, and cherish it.

TALK FIRST, BUY LATER

Build from the bottom up, not the top down. Hold community conversations to find out just what patrons are really interested in or really need, and have a solid understanding of what staff and volunteers are interested in and able to deliver. "Build it and they will come" might work well for a baseball field in a movie, but it's not a very solid business plan for a library makerspace. If your space doesn't have the equipment and programming that patrons are interested in, your makerspace might just be an empty space.

THINK GLOBALLY, BUILD LOCALLY

It's important to be aware of what other libraries are doing and the different types of programming and space development possible. But don't just do what other libraries have done. Do what works best for *your* library, in *your* community. Focus on your local questions and needs. The better tailored your space and programming is to your community, the more successful your space and programming will be.

EXPERTISE COUNTS

Although it's great to work with library colleagues, try to find experienced personnel whenever possible to help you honestly and expertly assess your needs and design your space. Sometimes these may be library professionals, sometimes outside professionals. Look at their track record, experience with libraries (if outside professionals), and history of collaboration.

GROW SUSTAINABLY

If long-term or permanent funding is difficult to secure, try funding project by project and set an intentional agenda for growth. Consider building out in stages, starting with community-driven creative programming to build interest and support and adding on equipment and other resources incrementally. Putting a 3D printer on a mobile cart and offering once-a-month 3D design classes can pique interest and generate enthusiasm more cost effectively than putting in a suite of printers and laser cutters no one has the interest or skills to use. Thoughtful growth reassures patrons and donors and can result in greater long-term financial sustainability and support.

DESIGN THE RIGHT SPACE FOR YOUR PLACE

If you feel confident customizing a small space in your library or repurposing larger spaces, a makerspace will probably serve your library and community well. If you want to be part of a dedicated network with established resources and protocols, you may want to consider setting up a FabLab instead. If you don't have the space or funding, pop-up makerspace programming might be best for your library.

Be educated about your options and flexible about exercising them, adapting space use and programming as patron and community needs and interests change or evolve.

INVEST WISELY

Equipment can vary widely in quality and reliability. Talk to other library makerspace organizers and read reviews to get a good understanding of the different types of printers, cutters, software, and other resources you're interested in. It's better to invest in one good machine or piece of equipment than several cheap ones, which will end up costing more in the long run due to repair or replacement costs.

FUND CREATIVELY

With financial support difficult to come by, don't overlook the value of in-kind contributions. Interested patrons or volunteers in the community may have woodworking skills that can translate into workbenches, 3D printer carts, or tool caddies. Others may be able to provide computer hardware or software support, teach classes, or donate equipment or supplies. Giving users the opportunity to give back with in-kind support also generates pride of ownership and commitment to your library.

Other ways to creatively sustain your makerspace can include naming rights, not just for rooms or your overall space but for equipment, too. Crowd funding can also be successful when targeted to specific needs like funding a piece of machinery. Instead of a gala, consider maker-style fundraising, like a gaming night or craft fair.

MANAGE RISK, BUT DON'T LET IT MANAGE YOU

Everyone wants to be on the cutting edge, but nobody wants to get cut. Putting a makerspace or FabLab in a library is a bit of a risk-taking venture. But nothing will stifle the success of a makerspace like overzealous risk management. Putting so many limitations and safety protocols in place that it becomes inconvenient and annoying to use the space negates any value the space brings to your library.

With reasonable precautions and good planning, however, the return on the investment of creative space and programming is much higher than the risk of serious injury or damage. Develop reasonable safety practices, display rules clearly, supervise responsibly, and make commonsense decisions about equipment, training, and usage so you can manage risk intelligently.

MAKE IT FUN!

In the long run, makerspaces, FabLabs, and maker-style programming are about making a joyful creative noise. We're inviting people to become active and empowered makers of their future, and of ours, in the heart of our communities, in our libraries, and that should be an enjoyable experience that people want to create and re-create again and again.

Celebrate your efforts with library maker festivals, gallery showings, library signage, newsletter and blog articles, and special events. Make it fun, and you'll make it successful and enduring!

7

FUTURE TRENDS

Throughout the course of this book, we've presented many examples of the close connection between libraries and making. Libraries clearly play a stimulating role in raising awareness of digital fabrication and the DIY culture. What does the future development of digital fabrication look like?

While this book was being written, the first 3D print in space was made.[1] And earlier in 2014, a young Dutch woman was fitted with a 3D-printed skull to overcome a life-threatening brain disorder.[2] These developments are taking place so rapidly that it is very difficult to make hard predictions. What can be said with certainty though is that digital manufacturing and the maker movement are changing the world little by little.

In 2014, Gartner, an information technology research and advisory company, released a hype cycle (trend report) about 3D printing.[3] Pete Basiliere, research vice president at Gartner, said, "Consumer 3D printing is around five to 10 years away from mainstream adoption. . . . Today, approximately 40 manufacturers sell the 3D printers most commonly used in businesses, and over 200 startups worldwide are developing and selling consumer-oriented 3D printers, priced from just a few hundred dollars. However, even this price is too high for mainstream consumers at this time, despite broad awareness of the technology and considerable media interest."

Interestingly, Gartner concludes that 3D printing still has a relatively long way to go before it will be a regular part of education. This is good news for libraries: Libraries can let users get acquainted with the technology and position themselves as strong partners of educational institutions. We're already seeing a lot of library makerspaces developing educational materials.

In September 2014, the broader concept of making was exhaustively documented in *The Maker's Manual*, a study by PSFK, an American trend research company, and Intel.[4] The report breaks the maker movement down into three basic themes:

- Democratized Creation, through the growing accessibility of DIY technology, "encouraging a greater number of people to become involved in the Maker Movement regardless of their knowledge and level of skill";
- Community Exchange, identifying the value of peer-to-peer sharing inherent in the maker community, "bringing people together to share essential knowledge and resources, while simultaneously creating new marketplaces for buying and selling their products"; and
- Growth Systems that help turn passions into products through new platforms and tools for funding, copyright management, and small-scale manufacturing.

All of these maker-driven innovations point toward a new industrial revolution, says Mark Hatch, CEO of TechShop: "When you move something from $1 million in development costs, or $250,000 in development costs, down to $5,000 you now enable anyone in the middle class to innovate. And that is new to the world. We've never operated, since the beginning of the industrial revolution, in an era where the middle class had access to the same kind of tools that the big boys do, and now they do."[5]

It is amazing to see how the maker movement has developed in recent years and exciting to think about where it will go next. Given its compatibility with the core values of librarianship, libraries can and should be a part of the developing story of the maker movement. The examples in this book show how growing numbers of libraries worldwide are taking their rightful place in the democratization of creation and twenty-first-century skills development, and we hope you feel inspired to be part of this promising future.

NOTES

1. Caleb Kraft, "First Successful 3D Print in Space Completed," *Make:*, November 25, 2014, http://makezine.com/2014/11/25/first-successful-3d-print-in-space-completed/ (accessed December 12, 2014).

2. Emily Thomas, "3D Printed Skull Saves Young Woman's Life," The Huffington Post, March 26, 2014, http://www.huffingtonpost.com/2014/03/26/3d-printed-skull-transplant-utrecht-_n_5036665.html (accessed December 12, 2014).

3. "Gartner Says Consumer 3D Printing Is More Than Five Years Away," Gartner, August 19, 2014, http://www.gartner.com/newsroom/id/2825417 (accessed December 7, 2014).

4. "Maker's Manual," PSFK, September 1, 2014, http://www.psfk.com/ (accessed December 12, 2014).

5. Jonathan O'Connell, "With TechShop, the Maker Movement Begins Its Rise in Washington," *Washington Post*, April 6, 2014, http://www.washingtonpost.com/news/capital-business/wp/2014/04/06/maker-movement-begins-rise-washington/ (accessed December 19, 2014).

RECOMMENDED READING

BOOKS

Abel, Bas Van. *Open Design Now: Why Design Cannot Remain Exclusive*. Amsterdam, The Netherlands: BIS Publishers, 2011.

Anderson, Chris. *Makers: The New Industrial Revolution*. New York: Crown Business, 2012.

Burke, John. *Makerspaces: A Practical Guide for Librarians*. Lanham, MD: Rowman & Littlefield, 2014.

Hatch, Mark. *The Maker Movement Manifesto: Rules for Innovation in the New World of Crafters, Hackers, and Tinkerers*. New York: McGraw-Hill, 2013.

Kemp, Adam. *The Makerspace Workbench: Tools, Technologies, and Techniques for Making*. Sebastopol, CA: Maker Media, 2013.

Lang, David, and Rebecca Demarest. *Zero to Maker: Learn (Just Enough) to Make (Just About) Anything*. San Francisco: Maker Media, 2013.

Lankes, R. David. *Expect More: Demanding Better Libraries for Today's Complex World*. Lexington, KY: R. David Lankes, 2012.

———. *The Atlas of New Librarianship*. Cambridge, MA: MIT Press, 2011.

Martinez, Sylvia Libow, and Gary Stager. *Invent to Learn: Making, Tinkering, and Engineering in the Classroom*. Torrance, CA: Constructing Modern Knowledge Press, 2013.

Wilkinson, Karen. *Art of Tinkering*. San Francisco: Weldon Owen, 2013.

ARTICLES

Britton, Lauren. "The Makings of Maker Spaces, Part 1: Space for Creation, Not Just Consumption—The Digital Shift." The Digital Shift. October 1, 2012. http://www.thedigitalshift.com/2012/10/public-services/the-makings-of-maker-spaces-part-1-space-for-creation-not-just-consumption/. Accessed December 6, 2014.

Colegrove, Todd. "Libraries as Makerspace?" Academia.edu. April 2, 2013. http://www.academia.edu/3041825/Libraries_as_makerspace. Accessed December 6, 2014.

De Boer, Jeroen. "Library as Maker and Informationspace." Medium. September 27, 2014. https://medium.com/@jtdeboer/library-as-maker-and-informationspace-c264ca4b2b36. Accessed December 6, 2014.

————. "Mobile Library Fab Lab Brings New Skills to Rural Areas." Opensource.com. June 2, 2014. http://opensource.com/education/14/5/mobile-library-fab-lab-brings-new-skills-rural-areas. Accessed December 6, 2014.

————. "Makerspaces Veroveren Hun Plaats in Bibliotheken." *InformatieProfessional*, June 1, 2013.

Enis, Matt. "To Remain Relevant, Libraries Should Help Patrons Create." The Digital Shift, Library Journal. May 25, 2012. http://www.thedigitalshift.com/2012/05/ux/to-remain-relevant-libraries-should-help-patrons-create/. Accessed December 6, 2014.

Ghikas, Mary. "American Library Association Supports Makerspaces in Libraries." American Library Association. October 6, 2014. http://www.ala.org/news/press-releases/2014/06/american-library-association-supports-makerspaces-libraries. Accessed December 6, 2014.

Hill, Nate. "Public Libraries | Multiple Solutions." Medium. July 30, 2014. https://medium.com/@natenatenate/public-libraries-multiple-solutions-ced2107026be. Accessed December 6, 2014.

Maker Media. "Makerspace Playbook." January 1, 2013. http://makered.org/wp-content/uploads/2014/09/Makerspace-Playbook-Feb-2013.pdf. Accessed December 6, 2014.

Mijnsbergen, Edwin. "Concept FabLab Verdient Het Verkend Te Worden." *Bibliotheekblad*, May 1, 2014.

Nygren, Ake. "The Public Library as a Community Hub for Connected Learning." IFLA 2014, Lyon. August 4, 2014. http://library.ifla.org/1014/1/167-nygren-en.pdf. Accessed December 6, 2014.

Shapiro, Phil. "A Librarian's Guide to Boosting the Maker Movement." *Make:*, August 28, 2013. http://makezine.com/2013/08/28/a-librarians-guide-to-boosting-the-maker-movement/. Accessed December 6, 2014.

Thompson, Clive. "Why Your Library May Soon Have Laser Cutters and 3-D Printers." Wired.com. August 31, 2014. http://www.wired.com/2014/09/makerspace/. Accessed December 6, 2014.

Willingham, Theresa. "The Library of the Future: Collaborative & Community Driven." Eureka! Factory. May 28, 2014. http://eurekafactory.net/2014/05/28/the-library-of-the-future-collaborative-community-driven/.

Young Adult Library Services Association. "Making in the Library Toolkit by the Makerspaces Resource Task Force." January 1, 2014. http://www.ala.org/yalsa/sites/ala.org.yalsa/files/content/MakingintheLibraryToolkit2014.pdf. Accessed December 6, 2014.

WEB RESOURCES

Business Models for Fab Labs: http://p2pfoundation.net/Business_Models_of_Fab_Labs
Common Library: http://commonlibraries.cc/resources/
Etsy Craft Entrepreneurship: http://craftentrepreneurship.com/
Fab Foundation: http://www.fabfoundation.org/fab-labs/what-is-a-fab-lab/
FabAcademy: http://www.fabacademy.org/
Google for Entrepreneurs: https://www.googleforentrepreneurs.com/
How to Make a Makerspace: http://artisansasylum.com/site/archiveclasses/make-a-maker space/
Libraries and Maker Culture: A Resource Guide: http://library-maker-culture.weebly.com/makerspaces-in-libraries.html
Marketing for Libraries: http://eduscapes.com/marketing/5.htm
Mt. Elliott Budget Worksheet and Other Financial Planning Resources: http://www.mtelliottmakerspace.com/finances
Tech Soup for Libraries: http://www.techsoupforlibraries.org/
Thinking outside the Brick: Lifelong Learning through Digital Play: http://dwig.lmc.gatech.edu/projects/farina/

Venture Lab Youth Entrepreneurship Program: http://venturelab.org/about/who-we-are/

INDEX

3D printing, 29–31, 32, 130; FreeFab3D Monolith, 47. *See also* seed bombs project
3D scanning, 31–32; software, 32

Aarhus Public Library (Denmark). *See* Folkelab
academic libraries, xiii, 2, 3. *See also* case studies; FabLab; Grand Center Arts Academy Charter School Library Makerspace
Adafruit, 34, 62. *See also* laser cutting
Adobe tools, 34, 42, 45, 52, 89, 91, 92
ALA. *See* American Library Association (ALA)
American Corner. *See* YouLab Pistoia (Italy)
American Library Association (ALA): Library of the Future, 41, 63; Loleta D. Fyan grant, 63. *See also* Make It @ Your Library
Amsterdam FabLab, 4
applications. *See* makerspaces
Arduino, 35, 87–88, 118n15. *See also* electronics; *Getting Started with Arduino* (book); robotics
Arizona State University. *See* Civic Center Library EUREKA cowork space
Artisan's Asylum, 5
arts, 70, 71, 75, 95, 109. *See also* Grand Center Arts Academy Charter School Library Makerspace
Arts Council England. *See* the Waiting Room
audio-video: hackathons, 112; THE HIVE, 45; Melrose Center, 42; YouLab, 51
autodesk, 32, 42. *See also* Instructables

Banzi, Massimo, 84. *See also Getting Started with Arduino* (book)
Bare Conductive Touch. *See* Hardware kits
Basiliere, Pete, 125. *See also* Gartner hype cycle
BiblioPT student created app, 47. *See also* YouLab Pistoia (Italy)
Bibliotheekservice Fryslân (Library Service Fryslân), 23, 53, 54. *See also* Fab the Library!; FrsykLab
Blikstein, Paulo, 78. *See also* seed bombs project
Blender 3D. *See* design software
Boeck, John, 24, 27n7
Britton, Lauren, 1, 6–7, 129. *See also* Fayetteville Free Library Fabulous Laboratory (Fab Lab)
budgeting, 18–19; See also business planning for makerspace; funding
build nights, 1, 14, 74. *See also* Instructables

Burke, John. *See* Makerspaces in Libraries Study
business: coworking space, 56; development, 108, 110; incubation, 2; support from, 64, 65, 106. *See also* cowork space; discovery sessions; entrepreneurship
business planning for makerspace, 19, 120; business model canvas, 55; business patterns, 27n8; FabLab Business Study, 24; for FabLab, 24, 27n9, 130; sustainability, 24. *See also* Empathy Mapping; FryskLab; makerspaces

CAD. *See* computer aided design (CAD)
call for makers, 76
Calavanti, Gui, 5. *See also* Artisan's Asylum
Carnegie UK Trust, 59, 67n9
case studies, 39–66
c-base, 2
Center for Bits and Atoms, 6. *See also* Gershenfeld, Neil
Chaos Communication Camp, 5
Civic Center Library EUREKA cowork space, 107, 118n23
Claesson, Lo. *See* Vaggeryd Library (Sweden)
Clark, Megan. *See* New Braunfels Public Library
Clark, Melody. *See* Fayetteville Free Library Fabulous Laboratory (Fab Lab)
clay circuits. *See* Squishy Circuits
clubs, 13, 67n10, 70; Geek Girls Club, 56. *See also* discovery sessions
CNC machines. *See* makerspaces, equipment
coding, 112, 116. *See also* computer programming
Colchester School of Art, 59
collaboration, 12, 36, 57, 66, 72, 141. *See also* hosting a hackathon, *FIRST* (For Inspiration and Recognition of Science and Technology), tips and tricks, seed bombs project
community engagement, 13, 15, 62; community conversations, 13–15, 120;

community partner inventory, 108. *See also* discovery sessions
Community Commons at Seminole Community Library, 47
community exchange, 126
computer programming, 35. *See also* getting started with Arduino (project); hackerspaces; hosting a hackathon
competitions.. *See* contests
computer aided design (CAD), 34; software for, 34. *See also* design software
Computer Science Education Week, 48
conductive dough. *See* Squishy Circuits
Considine, Sue. *See* Fayetteville Free Library Fabulous Laboratory (Fab Lab)
contests: Frysklab Open Product Design Challenges, 55; Instructables, 74, 77; maker contests, 73
Copenhagen FabLab, 58. *See also* Valby FabLab (Copenhagen, Demark)
cowork space, 107; in makerspace design, 17. *See also* Civic Center Library EUREKA cowork space
craft fair, 122; entrepreneurship, 106, 109; library projects, 71, 75; maker movement, 129; makerspaces, 2; senior makers, 102
creating an Entrepreneurship Center, 106–111. *See also* entrepreneurship
creating a simple laser-cut object project, 89–94. *See also* laser cutting
creative commons, 26, 52
creative programming, 13, 69, 121. *See also* Make It @ Your Library; senior makers
crowd funding, 9n9, 122; Donors Choose, 49; GoFundMe, 49
Cubiss consultancy office, 56–57
Cybraryman's Makerspace Resources, 37

Danak, Megan. *See* THE HIVE Community Innovation Center
data sources, 37; hackathon, 112, 113; metrics, 110. *See also* open data
De Boer, Jeroen, x, 67n4, 129, 130, 141. *See also* FryskLab
Democratized Creation, 126

design software, 29–30; CAD, 34; design repositories, 32; laser cutters, 34; modeling with, 83–72, 117n10; slicing, 30; Tinkercad, 29, 83, 117n10

digital commons, 8, 12, 54

digital fabrication: in Fab the Library!, 23–24, 32, 54, 117n8. *See also* FryskLab; future trends; Makersbuzz

digital literacy, 64, 102

discovery sessions, 13, 14, 16, 17, 18, 109

Disruption Department, 49. *See also* Goodin, Andrew; Grand Center Arts Academy Charter School Library Makerspace

DIY. *See* Do It Yourself (DIY)

documentation: Instructables, 77; makerspace, 19–20

Do It Yourself (DIY), 1; DIY Movement, 4

Dorothy Lumley Melrose Center for Technology, Innovation and Creativity (Orlando), 41–43, 102

Draftsight. *See* computer aided design (CAD)

Drawdio. *See* hardware kits

Dutch Institute for Public Libraries, 23

economic development, 15, 16, 107, 111, 118n24; Pasco Economic Development Council, 64, 108

Edgar Allan Ohms. *See FIRST* (For Inspiration and Recognition of Science and Technology)

education, 32, 37, 85, 117n8; 3D printing and, 125; activities, 26–13; Edutech Wiki, 32; FabLab, 25, 26; Makersbuzz, 57

electronics: Squishy Circuits, 101–105; tools and applications, 35. *See also* Arduino; littleBits electronic kits; Raspberry Pi

Empathy Mapping, 55

Entrepreneurial Librarianship, 106, 118n22

entrepreneurship, 118n23; Etsy Craft Entrepreneurship, 109, 110, 118n25, 130; Small Business Administration, 108; Small Business Day Celebration, 111; Small Business Resource collection, 111; start-ups, 106, 125; youth entrepreneurship, 109, 131. *See also* SCORE

Essex County Council Public Library Service, 59

EUREKA coworking space. *See* Civic Center Library EUREKA coworking space

Fab the Library!, 23–55. *See also* Bibliotheekservice Fryslân (Library Service Fryslân); FryskLab; mobile FabLab

FabLab, 1, 2, 6, 9n10, 9n11, 37; business models for, 24–27; FabLab Iceland Wiki page, 25; FabSchool, 36, 58; hands on training for, 23; International, 4, 23, 67n7; mobile, 41, 130. *See also* Boeck, John; Fab the Library!; Fayetteville Free Library Fabulous Laboratory (Fab Lab); FryskLab; Makersbuzz; Dorothy Lumley Melrose Center for Technology, Innovation and Creativity (Orlando); Troxler, Peter; Valby FabLab (Copenhagen, Demark)

facilities inventory, 16, 74–75

Farina, Kate, 102, 118n20, 130. *See also* senior makers

Fayetteville Free Library Fabulous Laboratory (Fab Lab), 40–41

FIRST (For Inspiration and Recognition of Science and Technology), 63–66; how to host a Jr. FLL team, 94–101; program comparison table, 96

focus groups. *See* discovery sessions

Folkelab, 61

FreeFab3D Monolith 3D Printer. *See* 3D printing

Friends of the Library: THE HIVE, 45; New Braunfels Public Library, 65

FryskLab, 23, 53–55, 67n5; Open Product Design Challenges, 55; See also FabLab; seed bombs project

Full Spectrum Laser. *See* laser cutting

fun, 123; *FIRST* programs, 64, 66, 94; Make It @ Your Library Day, 72; Pop-up Makerspace Programs, 73; Senior Maker Party, 106 funding, 121; creative funding, 122; potential sources, 19. *See also* grants; makerspaces

future trends, 125–126

GCAA Makerspace. *See* Grand Center Arts Academy Charter School Library Makerspace

gaming: creative fundraiser, 122; Game Night, 14; Indienomicon at Melrose Center, 42

Gartner hype cycle, 125, 127n3

Gershenfeld, Neil, 6. *See also* FabLab

Getting Started with Arduino (book), 35. *See also* getting started with Arduino (project)

getting started with Arduino (project), 84–88. *See also* Arduino

Goodin, Andrew. *See* Grand Center Arts Academy Charter School Library Makerspace

Grand Center Arts Academy Charter School Library Makerspace, 48–50

grants: FabLab, 25–26; *FIRST* grants, 64; IMLS grants, 19; Loleta D. Fyan grant, 63. *See also* funding

The Great Good Place, 7, 9n3. *See also* Oldenburg, Ray; the Third Place

guerilla gardening. *See* urban gardening

Hack Day. *See* hosting a hackathon

Hack Fest. *See* hosting a hackathon

Hackaday, 74, 117n4

hackathon. *See* hosting a hackathon

hacker, 4

hackerspaces, 5; history of, 2. *See also* makerspaces

hardware kits, 35–36

Haslet Public Library Robotics Club, 63. *See also* FIRST (For Inspiration and Recognition of Science and Technology)

Hatch, Mark, 126. *See also* TechShop

Hazel L. Incantalupo MakerSpace (Palm Harbor Library, Florida), 19

THE HIVE Community Innovation Center, 14, 43–46, 66n2

hosting a hackathon, 111–117

Illinois Libraries Explore, Apply and Discover (ILEAD), 69

IMLS. *See* Institute of Museum and Library Services (IMLS)

The Indus Entrepreneurs (TiE), 108

in-kind donations, 18, 41, 122. *See also* budgeting; funding

Innovation Lab. *See* St. Petersburg College Innovation Lab

Institute of Museum and Library Services (IMLS), 19, 27n3

Instructables, 32, 36, 74, 77, 117n1; LED project, 85, 87, 88, 117n13; step-by-step library projects, 69. *See also* Make It @ Your Library

insulating dough. *See* Squishy Circuits

Invent To Learn: Making, Tinkering, and Engineering in the Classroom, 37, 129

John F. Germany Public Library. *See* THE HIVE Community Innovation Center

Kendrick B. Melrose Family Foundation. *See* Dorothy Lumley Melrose Center for Technology, Innovation and Creativity (Orlando)

Kemp, Adam, 38, 90. *See also The Makerspace Workbench*

Kinect. *See* 3D scanning

Kootstra, Aan. *See* FryskLab

Kroski, Ellyssa, x

Land O' Lakes Branch Library, 15, 63. *See also FIRST* (For Inspiration and Recognition of Science and Technology)

Lankes, David, 56, 129

laser cutting, 33–34, 38n3, 90; design tools for, 34, 92–93; types of cutters, 33. *See also* Adafruit; creating a simple laser-cut object project

LED project. *See* getting started with Arduino (project)

Library as Incubator, 3, 9n4. *See also* Britton, Lauren

Library Box, 48

Library Makers website, 37

Library of San Giorgio di Pistoia (Italy).
See YouLab Pistoia (Italy)
Library of the Future, 11–12, 16, 130
library services: creative programming,
15; emerging technologies, 23; grants,
19; Library Services in the Digital Age
study, 12, 27n2
library staff: as stakeholders, 13;
community assessment, 21; FabLab
Training module, 23–27; in Library
Maker Projects, 69. See also Make It @
Your Library Day
littleBits electronic kits, 36, 117n7. See
also electronics

Made in the Library Fair, 73. See also
Make It @ Your Library Day
Madison Public Library. See Library
Makers website
Mairn, Chad.. See St. Petersburg College
Innovation Lab
Make and Take, 72
Make It @ Your Library, 36, 69–70, 71, 72
Make It @ Your Library Day, 69–73
Make: magazine, 2, 35, 37, 74
maker. See maker movement
Maker Boxes, 62–63
Maker Education Initiative. See education
Maker Festivals, 2; Gulf Coast
MakerCon, 141; library maker
festivals, 123; Maker Faire, 2; Maker
Faire history, 9n3; White House
Maker Faire, 4, 9n7
maker movement, 2, 4, 6, 7, 36, 125, 126,
127n5, 130. See also The Maker's
Manual; The Maker Movement
Manifesto
The Maker Movement Manifesto, 129
MakerBot. See 3D printing
Makersbuzz (Tilburg, the Netherlands),
56–57. See also FabLab
The Maker's Manual, 126
makerspace-in-a-box, 17. See also Maker
Boxes; pop-up makerspace
programming
The Makerspace Workbench, 38, 90,
118n16, 129
makerspaces, xiii, 1, 2–3, 6–7, 9n2, 9n12,
12, 27n5; American Library

Association, 130; different types, 4–6,
9n10; equipment, 29–36; handbook
and organizational documents, 19–22;
international makerspaces, 51–62;
space planning, 16–18; staff training,
23–24; sustainability, 24–27. See also
budgeting; business planning for
makerspaces; case studies; creative
programming; discovery sessions;
FabLab; funding; hackerspaces;
Makerspaces in Libraries Study; pop-
up makerspaces programming;
stakeholders; step-by-step projects;
tips and tricks
Makerspaces in Libraries Study, 3, 27n5
MaKey MaKey. See hardware kits
Massachusetts Institute of Technology
(MIT) Media Lab, 6. See also FabLab
McGarvey, Sean. See Pasco County
Library System
media literacy, 26; at FryskLab, 55
Medialiteracy Makers!, 55
Melrose Center. See Dorothy Lumley
Melrose Center for Technology,
Innovation and Creativity (Orlando)
mobile FabLab, 53. See also FryskLab;
Makersbuzz

National Day of Civic Hacking. See host-
ing a hackathon
Naylor, Annemarie. See the Waiting
Room
The Netherlands Institute for Public
Libraries (SIOB), 55. See also
FryskLab
New Braunfels Public Library, 65–66
Next Generation Science Standards, 49
Nygren, Åke. See makerspace-in-a-box;
Maker Boxes
Noisebridge, 2
NYC Resistor, 2, 5

Obama, Barack, 4. See also White House
Maker Faire
Oldenburg, Ray, PhD, 7, 9n13. See also
The Great Good Place; the Third Place
open data, 36
Open Design Now, 36

Orange County Library System (OCLS)
  Technology Training Program, 42
Orlando Public Library. *See* Dorothy
  Lumley Melrose Center for
  Technology, Innovation and Creativity
  (Orlando)
Overgaard, Louise. *See* Folkelab

Palm Harbor Library Hazel Incantalupo
  MakerSpace, 19
Pasco County Library System, 63
patrons, 1, 39, 130; introduction to maker
  programming, 17, 73; patron
  inventory, 109; senior patrons,
  101–102; stakeholders, 13–14, 18, 21.
  See also creative programming;
  discovery sessions; library services;
  step-by-step projects
Pew Research, 11, 27n1, 27n2; Library
  Services in the Digital Age, 12
pop-up makerspace programming, 17, 60,
  61, 73–78. *See also* Folkelab;
  makerspace-in-a-box
Prato, Stephanie, 106, 118n22
Project for Public Spaces, 8. *See also* the
  Third Place

Ranganathan Law, 53, 67n5
rapid prototyping. *See* 3D printing
Raspberry Pi, 35. *See also* hardware kits
Rasetti, Maria Stella. *See* YouLab Pistoia
  (Italy)
recommended reading, 129–131
Rendina, Diana, 37
risk management, 122. *See also* safety
robotics, 35. *See also* FIRST (For
  Inspiration and Recognition of Science
  and Technology); THE HIVE
  Community Innovation Center

safety, 20, 21, 122; agreements and
  policies, 22
Science Technology Activities and
  Resources Library Education
  Network, 63
SCORE, 108, 111
Scottsdale Public Library System Civic
  Center Library. *See* Civic Center
  Library EUREKA cowork space

Scratch, 35. *See also* computer
  programming
Schiller, Nicholas, 4, 9n8. *See also* hosting
  a hackathon
seed bombs project, 78–84, 117n9. *See
  also* 3D printing; urban gardening
simulation lab. *See* Dorothy Lumley
  Melrose Center for Technology,
  Innovation and Creativity (Orlando)
St. Petersburg College Innovation Lab,
  47–48
senior makers, 101–102, 106. *See also*
  Squishy Circuits; patrons
sewing machines. *See* makerspaces,
  equipment
simulation lab.. *See* Dorothy
step-by-step projects, 69–116. *See also*
  creating a simple laser-cut object
  project; creating an Entrepreneurship
  Center; getting started with Arduino
  (project); hosting a hackathon; seed
  bombs project; Make It @ Your
  Library Day; pop-up makerspace
  programming; Squishy Circuits
social media, 41, 77, 113
soldering. *See* makerspaces, equipment
Spark Fun. *See* hardware kits
sponsorship, 25, 64, 109. *See also* funding
Squishy Circuits, 101–106, 118n21
staff training, 23–24. *See also* step-by-step
  projects; Fab the Library!
stakeholders, 13–15, 60. *See also*
  discovery sessions
STAR Net. *See* Science Technology
  Activities and Resources Library
  Education Network
STEAM Innovation Lab. *See* Grand
  Center Arts Academy Charter School
  Library Makerspace
Stockholm Public Library (Sweden). *See*
  Makerspace in a Box
Stonebridge, Paul. *See* Land O'Lakes
  Branch Library
sustainability: environmental, 78; in
  FabLab development, 24, 27n7

Tampa-Hillsborough County Public
  Library System. *See* THE HIVE Community Innovation Center

TechShop, 2, 9n10, 126, 127n5. *See also*
    Hatch, Mark
teen advisory board, 14. *See also* patrons
TiE. *See* The Indus Entrepreneurs (TiE)
Tinkercad. *See* design software
tips and tricks, 119–123
Thingiverse, 32, 36. *See also* 3D printing
the Third Place, 7–8, 10n14, 10n15
tools. *See* makerspaces, equipment
Troxler, Peter, 24–25

Ultimate Guide to 3D Printing, 30
University of St. Thomas. *See* Squishy
    Circuits
urban gardening, 80

Vaggeryd Library (Sweden), 56
Valby FabLab (Copenhagen, Demark),
    58–59
Van Helvoort, Neeltje. *See* Makersbuzz
Vengersammy, Ormilla. *See* Dorothy
    Lumley Melrose Center for
    Technology, Innovation and Creativity
    (Orlando)
Vestergaard, Rasmus Fangel. *See* Valby
    FabLab (Copenhagen, Demark)

ventilation, 18; in workspace
    configuration, 71; laser cutting, 90
Venture Lab Youth Entrepreneurship
    Program, 131. *See also*
    entrepreneurship
volunteers, 102; as stakeholders, 13;
    senior volunteers, 80, 102; See also
    discovery sessions; makerspaces

the Waiting Room (Colchester, UK),
    59–60, 67n9
Ward-Crixell (kit). *See* New Braunfels
    Public Library
web design: in hackathon, 112; Mozilla
    Webmaker, 55
White House Maker Faire, 4, 9n7. *See
    also* Obama, Barack
Willingham, Theresa, 66n2, 130, 141

YouLab Pistoia (Italy), 51–53
youth patrons, 5, 13; in YouLab, 51. *See
    also* discovery sessions; *FIRST* (For
    Inspiration and Recognition of Science
    and Technology); patrons; teen
    advisory board; Venture Lab Youth
    Entrepreneurship Program